The
Aquariums
of
Pyongyang

Author (right), age 19, one year after his release from the Yodok labor camp with (left to right) his third uncle, sister Mi-ho, grandmother, and third aunt.

BASIC
BOOKS

A Member of the Perseus Books Group

THE
AQUARIUMS
OF
PYONGYANG

Ten Years in a North Korean Gulag

강철환

Kang Chol-hwan
and
Pierre Rigoulot

Translated by Yair Reiner

Originally published in 2000 in France as
Les Aquariums de Pyongyang by Éditions
Robert Laffont

Translation copyright © 2001 by
Kang Chol-hwan and Pierre Rigoulot

Published by Basic Books,
A Member of the Perseus Books Group

Designed by *Brent Wilcox*

A cataloging-in-publication record for this
book is available from the Library of Congress.
ISBN 0–465–01101–2

01 02 03 04 / 10 9 8 7 6 5 4 3 2 1

CONTENTS

서문

INTRODUCTION
North Korea—the World's Last Stalinist Regime

November 1999. Weighed down by jet lag and four hours of interviewing, I let myself be driven around in silence. Kang Chol-hwan slips his favorite CD into the car stereo. "La Paloma" comes on, then "Nathalie," played to the melody of "Yeux noirs." He turns it up a notch. The music flowing from the two black speakers seems to inspire him. The audio system in his car must have cost him plenty; the sound quality is superb. I watch him smile and smooth-ly shift gears, mindful of not breaking the spell.

Before I know it we're in Apkujong, the neighborhood where ado-lescents with too much money stroll into Gucci's and Lacroix.

Red light.

Night has fallen by the time we pass Ciné House and The Muses, the fine restaurant where patrons once dined by candle-light, regaled by live operetta. I wonder why it's closed down. Kang Chol-hwan slowly accelerates as we head up toward the Amiga Hotel. The apartment of our interpreter, Song Okyung, is only a few hundred yards away.

We're in Seoul, Korea's historic capital of 14 million inhabitants. Kang Chol-hwan has an e-mail account; he surfs the Internet; he skis; he worries about his Hyundai stocks. Kang Chol-hwan speaks Korean. He writes Korean using *han'gul*, a twenty-four-letter alphabet of ten vowels and fourteen consonants invented five centuries ago by King Se-jong.

In a word, he's Korean. Yet he's not from here. He comes from another country, one that's also called Korea, but where no one drives Daewoos. No one has a stereo in their car. In the countryside, oxen draw pushcarts. There's no Internet. No glossy magazines with pictures of gorgeous girls. No newspapers with different points of view. No chance to choose between the ten or twenty available radio signals, because the dial is permanently set to the official government station. One government channel on the television. To move around the country, a citizen first needs to get permission from the Party, then from the head of his or her work unit.

Kang Chol-hwan comes from the North, meaning north of the demilitarized zone that separates North and South Korea. The zone— four and a half miles wide and 150 miles long—outlines an enormous wound running through the heart of the Korean peninsula. Its two edges are lined with more than 300 miles of barbed wire, fencing, and antipersonnel mines, all keeping the country separated from itself.

How can Koreans stand this?

They can't. They are all more or less sickened by this separation. Imagine this metallic barrier in America: if we take, for example, the thirty-sixth parallel as a boundary line, it would separate Nashville from Memphis and Oklahoma City from Tulsa. Raleigh-Durham and Greensboro–Winston-Salem would be turned into opposing border cities right in the middle of North Carolina.

Only the Germans can fathom the horror of such a rending, of people shot trying to flee, of artificially divided worlds becoming hostile to their core. Yet even between the two Germanys a few points of passage did exist; a few exchanges were possible. Eastern Germans could at least watch Western television broadcasts. In Korea, the separation is absolute: on one side are Koreans; on the other . . . also Koreans. Yet each side keeps to itself. Both countries forbid any crossing. If you have a brother in the North, you won't hear from him. If you live here and your mother lives there, you would do well to forget about her for the time being. But don't worry: the demilitarized zone probably has more soldiers per square foot than anywhere on the planet.

The states that lay down the law on each side of this rupture were created in 1948. After a colonial period that lasted for a generation—from 1910 to 1945—and ended when Imperial Japan crumbled under America's atom bombs, Korea, much to the dismay of its citizens, was split in two. Its north was occupied by Soviet troops, the south by Americans.

Split is perhaps not the right word. Initially it was a matter of a double administration, a provisional guardianship designed to last until elections could be organized under the aegis of the United Nations. But elections weren't held. They were never held. The rival administrations clashed, over which parties should be allowed to present themselves, over election dates, over the number of elected representatives. The disputes and delays served Stalin well, for he had no intention of withdrawing quickly. He was training a cadre of submissive political leaders in the north, building up an army, and organizing a well-publicized movement for agrarian reform by setting the poorest peasants against their landlords and rousing the support of numerous leftist parties around the world.

Stalin's men had hardly undertaken to effect agrarian reform, when the hour for collectivization was ripe.

All this time the United Nations was growing impatient. Meetings gave birth to conferences, accusatory communiqués to bittersweet responses—but 1945 ended without action, then 1946, too. A wave of refugees flowed from the northern to the southern zones. By 1947, it had became harder to flee. The Soviet-American military fraternity that had so recently battled fascism was now a distant memory. The cold war had begun.

The boundary between the two zones gradually became something akin to a border. To its north, "people's committees" were formed and began drawing the outlines of a new state. In the south, the less enterprising Americans, who had chosen to build up a huge police force rather than a powerful army—as their Soviet rivals had done—were making little effort to create a government in their image, opting instead to leave power in the hands of the same bourgeoisie that had been compromised during occupation by its relations with the Japanese. Although Americans hadn't any great reforms to trumpet, they did have the backing of the UN, and in the face of Soviet opposition to holding countrywide elections, they organized their own vote in the South. The elections, which were anything but general, left half the National Assembly seats unfilled. The Republic of Korea nevertheless was born. It elected Rhee Syng-man, an upright man who had fought against Japanese occupation, as president of the assembly. This was in August 1948. The response from the North came quickly. The following month, in Pyongyang, the northern zone's largest city, the Democratic People's Republic was proclaimed, with Kim Il-sung, a former local guerilla leader who had fought against the Japanese in Manchuria, at its head. Kim Il-sung was presiding over what was already a full-fledged state, rebuilt from roof to baseboard and equipped with a police force and army hefty enough to allow the Soviet army to pull out in the autumn of 1948, thereby depriving the American military presence in the South of its legitimacy. By the end of the following winter, the Americans were out, too.

What follows did not come fully to light until 1994, when Boris Yeltsin opened up the related Soviet archives. Kim Il-sung, it appears, was stamping his feet in impatience. He wanted immediately to throw his army into an assault on the South, which was poorly armed, poorly organized, and suffering under the harshest economic difficulties—not to mention harassed by a northern-backed guerilla movement. Prudent as always, Stalin waited another few months before giving the green light. On June 25, 1950, despite assurances from observers that an attack from the North was almost unthinkable, North Korean tanks broke through the line of demarcation along the thirty-eighth parallel. Seoul fell in three days, as the North Korean army stormed its way down the peninsula, making short work of Rhee Syng-man's small South Korean army and its several hundred American advisors. North Korea soon controlled 90 percent of the peninsula.

This was the start of the Korean War, a conflict of incredible reversals. The American president, Harry Truman, reacted quickly. Standing before the UN Security Council, he denounced North Korea's premeditated aggression and pleaded for the young international organization to respond with "all its means." The UN's decision was made all the easier by the Soviet Union's sulky protest to the organization's admittance of Chiang Kai-shek's China into the Security Council. On June 27, the UN called on its member nations to lend military assistance to South Korea. On September 15, American forces under the command of General MacArthur landed in the rear of the North Korean army. Caught off guard, Pyongyang's troops fled or were destroyed. Under the blue-and-white banner of the UN, the American and South Korean troops, joined now by contingents from Turkey, England, France, and the Netherlands, liberated the capital, penetrated the North, took Pyongyang, and made their way up toward the Amnok River. Known to both the Chinese and Americans as the Yalu, the river marked the northwest border between Korea and the People's Republic of China.

Mao Tse-tung responded by throwing several hundred thousand volunteers into battle. The UN troops suffered heavy losses and were forced to beat a hasty retreat. The seesaw battle again had changed course: Pyongyang was abandoned, UN troops fell below the thirty-eighth parallel, and Seoul was abandoned. After five months of fierce battle, the front stabilized. The scale then gradually began tipping in the other direction: Seoul was recaptured for the second time and the battle line pushed a bit farther north.

On July 27, 1953, three years and one million deaths after Kim Il-sung's surprise attack and shortly on the heels of Stalin's death, an armistice was signed in the village of Panmunjom.

The United Nations prevented a takeover, but failed to reunify the country.

One day I met a North Korean soldier who had recently defected to the South and was still recovering from the shock. He asked me, almost pleading, to clear something up for him.

"Who won the Korean War?" he wanted to know. "Here they claim the opposite of what I was told in the North!"

What could I tell him?

Tie game would have been a fair answer, given that the two armies ended up more or less where they started. That would have seemed too flip, however, and the question had been posed in earnest. Should I have said that both sides lost? That's certainly true if one considers the untold misery caused by the war and the hundreds of thousands who died. Yet such a reply would have ignored the subsequent development of South Korea, which only was made possible by pushing back the Communist forces.

Until it began a process of democratization in 1987, South Korea was effectively run as an authoritarian—and sometimes dictatorial—regime. Since 1960, it nevertheless has presided over an unprecedented economic boom. Thirty years of unflagging effort has lifted South Korea's economy from Bangladeshi levels to parity with Spain. The packed-earth roads of Seoul, where little girls once sold their hair, have seen the skyline fill with skyscrapers and the streets jam with cars, most painted metallic silver, and almost all equipped with hi-fi stereos and air-conditioning *made in Korea*. In very little time, South Korea has grown into the world's seventh industrial power.

During this period, forty kilometers to the north, an ideological and military hedgehog was being formed, sometimes with the patronage of Mao's China, sometimes with that of Brezhnev's USSR, but always under the absolute control of one man: Kim Il-sung. His bloody purges in the 1980s cleared the way for the succession of his son, Kim Jong-il, and helped establish the world's first Communist dynasty.

Political and economic relations between North Korea and the "capitalist" South remained embryonic, while occasional quasi-military strikes continued to smolder and flare: in 1968, commandos raided the Blue House (the presidential palace in Seoul); in 1981, a delegation of South Korean government officials came under attack while visiting the Burmese capital of Rangoon; in 1987, a (South)

Korean Airlines jet exploded in midair; in 1994, there were submarine intrusions and further commando raids; in 1999, it was a sea battle, and so forth.

In North Korea, a country of 22 million, the police survey every aspect of the citizenry's life. No travel without authorization. No news that's not vetted first. A single, mandated ideology, exalting self-sufficiency—even when calling for international aid. Extensive prisons and camps scattered throughout the country. Its economy, modeled after Stalin's Soviet Union—controlled, centralized, collectivized—crumbled in the 1970s and 1980s and collapsed heavily with the fall of communism in the Soviet Union, the reforms in China, and the death in 1994 of the Great Leader Kim Il-sung.

Famine gradually has spread across the country, and there's talk of 3 million dead. Today North Korea is a ship in distress, slowly sinking beneath the waves. Thanks to substantial handouts from the international community, the state—which is really just a party—can save the hard currency it should be using to purchase produce on the international market.

North Korea's leaders prefer to invest their limited resources in the development of sophisticated armaments. Their missiles are sold in Iran and Syria, and their longest-range model soon will have the capacity of reaching the United States. With understandably little desire to see the Korean peninsula destabilize the region, interested powers seek to mollify Kim Jong-il, convinced—though it's unclear why—that he can be seduced and even persuaded to see the virtues of political democracy and economic liberalism. The recent show put on by Kim Il-sung's son—who's a great fan of the movies—in which he appeared smiling and cheerful in his June 12, 2000, summit meeting with Kim Dae-jung, the South Korean president, has done nothing to change the base facts. After the summit, as before, North Korea's population continues to die of hunger and suffer from a total absence of political freedom. Children are stunted, thousands of young women are sold across the border in China, and the army parades through the streets of Pyongyang, ever ready to protect its fantastical socialist paradise.

A few have managed to flee. Kang Chol-hwan is one of them. He left North Korea in 1992, before the famine reached its peak. He didn't leave the country to escape the famine, as so many do today, but because having once survived imprisonment in concentration camp number 15, he was in danger of being arrested again, this time for "listening to banned radio."

Though it reaches a Western audience somewhat late, his testimony represents the first extended account of a young adult's life in contemporary North Korea. This is the first detailed testimony about a North Korean concentration camp to be published in the West.

I first met Kang Chol-hwan in Seoul shortly after his defection. I was visiting South Korea regularly as part of my work for the International Organization for Human Rights, interviewing renegades about repression in North Korea. Convinced that North Korea had gained as much from its own population's ignorance of the outside world as from the international public's ignorance of its crimes and threats against its own population, I suggested to Kang Chol-hwan that he tell the Western world what it was like to live under the rule of Kim Il-sung and his son, Kim Jong-il. He accepted, seeing it as his moral duty to shed light on the horrors of the Pyongyang regime and, above all, its system of concentration camps.

We met five or six times in Seoul, shutting ourselves up in a hotel room and breaking only for lunch and dinner. We communicated by the intermediary of a South Korean academician, a specialist in French literature, whose role was both essential and irreplaceable. Her modesty was equaled only by her effectiveness in helping me understand the intricacies of the country as a whole, as well as North Korea's particular contempt for human rights.

This book thus results from the efforts of three people, working together as friends, with the common hope of raising international awareness. All those who would deal with North Korea—be they diplomats, politicians, businessmen—should know that their interlocutor is the planet's last Stalinist regime, a regime that incarcerates between 150,000 and 200,000 people in concentration camps, flouts freedom of conscience, mercilessly clubs its population with pompous, mendacious propaganda, and is responsible for one of the worst famines of the end of the twentieth century. The most fitting term to describe it has already been coined, but I will employ it here again: the regime is ubuesque. Which is to say grotesque and bloody.

Reading this book is a first step toward making the repression in North Korea a major concern for human rights defenders around the world.

Pierre Rigoulot

하나

ONE

A HAPPY CHILDHOOD IN PYONGYANG

In the 1960s, North Korea's disaster was not yet on the horizon. In economic terms, the country was going neck and neck with the South, and in Pyongyang, the regime's privileged showcase, it seemed the Party's talk of triumph and promise might actually hold true. I know what I'm talking about; Pyongyang is where I was born and grew up. I even lived some happy years there, under the guardian eye of Kim Il-sung, our "Great Leader," and his son, Kim Jong-il, our "Dear Leader."

To the child I was, Kim Il-sung was a kind of Father Christmas. Every year on his birthday, he would send us gift packages of cakes and sweets. Our beloved Number One chose them himself, with a care and kindness that gave his gifts a savoriness all their own. Thanks to his generosity, we also had the right, every third year, to a school uniform, a cap, and a pair of shoes.

Our mothers said these polyester uniforms were sturdy, easy to wash, and permanently pressed. As for the shoes, daily use showed them to be of excellent quality. The ceremony for the distribution of uniforms, a most solemn event, was held in the large hall adjoining the school, which was specially decorated for the occasion with slogans and portraits. The parents in attendance applauded speeches by the school principal and several representatives of the Party. Student delegates got on the rostrum and thanked the Party in their little childish voices, pledging allegiance to the Clairvoyant, and pouring imprecations on all our enemies, American imperialism first among them, "because its claws still grip part of our dear Fatherland." At the end, the student delegates were entrusted with the precious gifts, which they distributed to the rest of the pupils the following day.

Kim Il-sung was actually even better than Father Christmas, because he seemed eternally young and omniscient. Like his son, Kim Jong-il, who was said to be in line to succeed him, he was more like a god to us than Father Christmas. The newspapers, the radio, posters, our textbooks, our teachers: everyone and everything seemed to confirm this. By marrying our singular Korean genius with the immutable ideals of the Communist revolution, these two masterminds, these two darlings of the universe, were building for us the Edenic socialist state. Had not Kim Il-sung's political acumen and incomparable intellect already been the cause of wonders, against the cruel American invaders, for example, whom he dealt the most humiliating of defeats? Only much later did I learn how the war was really started and what happened in its aftermath. Like millions of other North Korean children, I was taught that thanks to the military genius of our Great Guide and, to a lesser degree, the international aid of China, to whom we were united "like lips to teeth," our

valiant People's Army had routed the Americans. Kim Il-sung—
a.k.a. the Light of Human Genius, the Unequaled Genius, the
Summit of Thought, the North Star of the People—was the object
of a personality cult extravagant enough to rival that of Stalin or
Mao Tse-tung, and indeed, even to outlive them. In 1998, the
People's Supreme Assembly even made the astounding decision to
name Kim Il-sung president "for all eternity"—four years after his
death!

To my childish eyes and to those of all my friends, Kim Il-sung
and Kim Jong-il were perfect beings, untarnished by any base
human function. I was convinced, as we all were, that neither of
them urinated or defecated. Who could imagine such things of
gods? In the portraits of their paternal faces I found comfort and all
that was protecting, kindly, self-assured.

Like other children, I started grammar school at the age of six—or
seven, if you count according to the traditional Korean formula,
where year one begins at conception and another year is added
every January 1. (The Korean and Western calculus for determining
age can vary by as many as two years.) While ordinarily eager to
defend its traditions, North Korea has officially renounced this
manner of calculating age, although it is still widely used in private.

The name of the grammar school I attended was the School of
the People, and Kim Il-sung once honored it with a visit—a truly
exceptional event, which conferred the greatest prestige on the
parents whose children attended the institution. Of this place, too,
I have fond memories. I recall with particular warmth Mrs. Ro
Chong-gyu, a teacher of enormous kindness and pedagogical skill,
who always found the right word to encourage me. Despite their
adherence to communist educational methods, almost all the

teachers I had were attentive and patient with their pupils, even during our criticism and self-criticism sessions. Anyone who has never lived in a Communist country may be shocked at the thought of little children mimicking their politicized elders and denouncing themselves and others for lacking revolutionary vigilance or for not meriting the Great Leader's confidence. Yet these sessions generally ended with words of encouragement from our teachers, not of reproach, and with the hope that we would try harder in the future. I don't believe any of us were really traumatized by these sessions.

To help initiate us into North Korea's highly militaristic brand of communism, we were awarded different ranks at school. We were hardly seven years old when our uniforms first began bearing stars—two or three, depending on our level. Already we were being directed by a "political leader," the number one of the class, and by a delegate, the number two, who were appointed by the teacher and confirmed by a vote of the pupils. Admittedly, I was never much taken with military discipline: one day I convinced about fifteen of my classmates to ditch school and go to the zoo. It didn't take long to notice fifteen absentees, and the episode soon caused a big stir. Since I was the class delegate, I was not only publicly demoted but was expected to execute my self-criticism with deeper-than-usual compunction and with exceptionally good form.

In the curriculum, too, training the revolution's little soldiers was given first priority. Like students everywhere in the world, we learned to read and write with as few mistakes as possible; we studied arithmetic, drawing, music, performed gymnastics, and so on. But above all, we were taught about the morals of communism and the history of the revolution of Kim Il-sung and Kim Jong-il. Given its singular import, the latter subject demanded that we learn by rote answers to questions such as: On what day and at what hour was Kim Il-sung born? What heroic feats did he perform against the Japanese? What speech did he give at such-and-such a conference, on such-and-such date? Like my fellow pupils, I thought cramming myself with such important facts was perfectly normal, and doing it gave me great pleasure. An education of this sort resulted in a well-spring of admiration and gratitude for our political leaders and in the willingness to sacrifice everything for them and the homeland. Like everyone in my class, I signed up for the Pupils' Red Army. What a sight we must have made marching into battle, fake machine guns slung across our shoulders. Though we mostly just learned to form ranks and sing while marching, we loved these exercises and never had to be asked twice to strike a military pose. Right away we felt we were Kim Il-sung's little soldiers. We were never asked to do anything too demanding. The training was adapted to our tender age and generally consisted of marching around the schoolyard a few times or around a block of houses. It wasn't until the penultimate year of high school that we would be allowed to undertake the more serious and difficult exercises. The high school students went on mountain hikes, memorized emergency air-raid instructions, learned to hide from enemy planes, and to steer the population to the nearest air-raid shelters.

When I wasn't in school, I could usually be found playing outside with the kids in my neighborhood. My favorite thing was to meet up under the weeping willows that ran along the Daedong River not far from where I lived. My friends and I knew the place well and felt completely safe there. At regular intervals we could hear a nearby bell, whose ringing had gradually become an integral part of the landscape. In warm weather, we waded in the water, catching dragonflies and other insects. And winter could be just as wonderful, during the festive time in late December, for example, when the statues of Kim Il-sung were decorated with footlights and draped with banners wishing us a happy New Year. Winter break ran from December 31 to mid-February, and when we tired of snowball fights, we would go back to our beloved river to ice-skate or play a game of ice hockey.

It would be bad grace to deny I had a happy childhood, but my family was better off than most, living in a newly built neighborhood that was exceptionally quiet, airy, and verdant. Situated near the main train station, Kyongnim-dong might have been less beautiful than the perimeter areas reserved for the nomenklatura, but it certainly came a close second. In my mind's eye, I remember it more as a park than as an urban neighborhood. Our apartment was large enough to comfortably accommodate all seven of us: my parents; my little sister, Mi-ho, whose name means "beautiful lake" and who is two years my junior; my paternal grandparents; one of my uncles—my "third uncle," according to Korean usage, which ranks uncles and aunts according to age and hierarchical standing; and me. My family enjoyed a level of comfort foreign to most North Korean homes, even in Pyongyang. We had a refrigerator, washing machine, vacuum cleaner, and even the most sought-after of all luxury goods: a color television set, on which, to our great delight, we could watch the dramatic political-crime series "Clean Hands." Even our clothes seemed rich compared to those of our neighbors, to whom my grandmother would often give away what we no longer needed.

There was no real poverty in our neighborhood or anywhere else—at least in the big cities. North Korea hadn't yet begun to suffer the major food and energy shortages it knows today. The rationing system worked well, and at the beginning of every month families received coupons for procuring food and heating oil. At our house, things were even better. My grandfather, who held a supervisory position in the state's goods distribution network, had access to almost anything, including nearly unlimited supplies of meat. People privileged enough to know this important man sometimes dropped by for a visit only to depart with a little something extra in the bottom of their bag, a supplement to the rations provided by the government.

Other images from that time come back to me. We lived a few dozen steps from the Soviet embassy, and children of the diplomatic corps sometimes ventured onto what my comrades and I considered *our* territory. We watched with hostile curiosity as the group of foreign-tongued blond children walked through our neighborhood. We would harass them and try to pull their hair, and they'd push us aside or run away; but somehow the clumsy overtures never broke out into a general melee. Yet when it came to fighting among ourselves, we never let an opportunity slip. I was a difficult child—stubborn, vindictive, determined—never missing an opportunity to measure myself up against a competitor. My fights were sometimes stopped by my grandfather, who absolutely adored me. If I was on the short end of a brawl, he would break it up and call both me and my adversary hooligans, but whenever he saw I had the upper hand, he stayed out of it—beaming with pride.

In North Korea, kids my age were encouraged to cultivate a spirit of competition. I remember a time when students in every class posted numbers representing their relative position in terms of physical strength. The various classes then organized fights to measure their number one against the number one of other classes.

Koreans can be violent, but they are also saccharine sentimental-
ists, who are easily brought to tears by the soppiest songs and most
mawkish novels. I therefore hope I will be forgiven for cherishing
another memory, this one of a little six-year-old girl. I was seven
years old and I thought she was beautiful. So did a movie director,
who spotted her and put her in one of his movies. She must have
liked me as much as I liked her, because for a long time we were
inseparable. "We'll be marrying you two before long," my grandmother once joked.

The prediction delighted the little girl but threw me into a violent
rage. Why such fury? Perhaps my grandmother had unintentionally
hit on a tender spot. Sex was a taboo subject in the North Korean
educational system, and maybe in my mind as well. Was my anger
an attempt to mask my embarrassment? Whatever the reason, that
first love meant a lot to both me and the little girl: years later, when
she was in high school and I was in the camp, she dared to inquire
about my well-being. I went to visit her when I finally got out, but
it was too late. Ku Bon-ok—the "real jewel" that the definition of
her name rightly presaged—had married and moved away. To where
I never learned.

I had one other childhood love: aquarium fish. Raising pigeons
was the more popular hobby among my friends, but that never did it
for me. My thing was fish, and they were more important to me than
anything. Even sitting in class and listening to my teacher, I was with
them in my thoughts. I worried that they were bored without me,
that their water was at the wrong temperature, that an evildoer had
broken into the house and done something to them. Almost all the
kids I knew had an aquarium, but coming from a well-to-do family,
I had about ten of them lining the walls of my room. As luck had it,
not far from us was a store that sold water plants, colored pebbles,

and other accessories. To make sure I always had the most original merchandise, I would wake up early and be the first to arrive upon opening. The lady who ran the store liked her assiduous young client and paid me a big smile every time I came and asked, in my most serious nine-year-old manner, to reserve such-and-such species from the next shipment of fish.

I wanted to own the most beautiful fish in the neighborhood, and the biggest and the strangest. One day I had the idea of adding specimens from the neighboring river to my collection. The trick had never been tried. So I caught a few fish, quickly brought them home, dropped them into an aquarium, and ran back out to fetch my friends so they could admire my new acquisitions. But alas, by the time we returned, the new lodgers had departed this world.

The competition for aquarium fish was as stiff as for physical strength, and jealousy gnawed at us whenever someone got a fish more beautiful than our own. One time a kid in my neighborhood invited us over to see an exotic fish he had just received as a gift, a truly magnificent specimen with huge bulging eyes. Yet no sooner had the boy owner stepped away from the aquarium, when one of his guests plunged a hand into the water and ripped out one of the fish's eyes. The fish was too beautiful to live in someone else's aquarium.

TWO

MONEY AND THE REVOLUTION CAN GET ALONG

My family's relative wealth was due not only to my grandparents' social status but also to the fact that they had once lived and prospered in Japan. My grandmother was the first to exile herself there. She was born near the southern tip of the Korean peninsula, on the island of Cheju, famous for its windy weather, its horses, and the strong character of its women. To this day you see them on television wearing wetsuits and diving into the ocean in search of shellfish, while their men stay home minding the children.

On older maps, the island often appears under the name of Quellepart. The appellation originated with the arrival of a group of French missionaries, who asked everyone they saw *en quelle partie*—

in which part—of Korea they had landed.* Whether called Quellepart or Cheju, it's the largest of the many islands scattered around the Korean coast, and in recent years it has developed into a major tourist site. In fact, it's now the number one destination among South Korean newlyweds, who flock there on their honeymoons.

In the 1930s, though, life on the island was very difficult. Much of the population emigrated to Japan, to find work at the center of the colonial empire to which Korea had belonged since 1910.

Grandmother was the third daughter in a poor household, where a typical meal consisted of sweet potatoes, occasionally accompanied by fish. At age thirteen, she left the island for Japan. It seems she was an intelligent child. She told me with a laugh that when she was young her father always said, "Ah, if you'd been a boy, you really could have been somebody."

She set out on her own, intending to find work in a textile factory in Kyoto. As it turned out, she came up an inch or so short. The factory owners weren't allowed to hire anyone under the age of thirteen, and since girls never had any identification papers, factory owners had to judge age solely on the basis of height. A bit short for her age, my grandmother was told to come back after she had grown a little. Still, she didn't want to go back to Korea. She begged in the streets for a time and slept in the factory dormitory, where a few workers from back home had taken her under their wing. She told me most of her food came from poulterers, who gave her the chicken heads their customers didn't want. I have the impression that wasn't the worst of it, either. She lived that way for a year, until she grew another inch or two and was hired by the factory. The

*This name is encountered in the journal of Hamel, a seventeenth-century Dutch sailor, who lived in Korea for a time. He gives the spelling as Quelpaert. This spelling appears on a number of maps. (All the notes in this book are Pierre Rigoulot's.)

work was hard, but she liked it. She was proud to earn her first wages and shortly repaid the girls who had helped her out. What little money was left over she sent back home to her family.

The Socialist movement was gaining ground in Japan, especially among teachers. So it is no surprise that Grandmother was first introduced to the ideas of socialism by her night school instructor. My grandmother was a bright student, attentive, curious, quick to learn. Several of her teachers grew attached to her and, through their discussions, tried to direct the young, upright girl toward socialism.

She joined the Japanese Communist Party at age twenty, which was around the same time she met her husband-to-be, who was, like her, a native of Cheju. The oldest of three children, he had set out for Japan to extricate himself from an ill-begotten marriage arranged by his parents. He was fifteen years old at the time, his wife about the same. The two young people never loved each other, and the marriage quickly proved a failure. Eventually my grandfather decided to run away, leaving his wife back home with his parents. According to Confucian tradition, which continues to hold sway in present-day Korea, a married woman belongs to her husband's family and remains so, irrespective of divorce or separation. If she tries to return to her parents' home, she will most likely be turned away.

My grandfather had a more auspicious landing in Japan than did my grandmother. Within a short time, he found work in a jeweler's shop and learned gold plating. After quickly mastering the technique, he established his own shop to manufacture novelty jewelry. About that time he met my grandmother. The man who wanted to make a fortune and the woman who wanted to make revolution fell in love and married. My father was their first child. In 1934, the couple traveled back to Cheju and moved in with my grandfather's family, a step that may shock the Western mindset, but that was not at all rare in Korea. The first wife had no choice but silently to endure the presence of the new wife under the same roof.

Their return was short-lived. My grandparents soon were on their way back to Japan. In the meantime, however, Grandmother made the best of her sojourn on Cheju. In her fervor she managed to expand substantially the number of Communist contacts and help organize numerous discussion groups and meetings on the island. For my grandfather, on the other hand, revolutionary ideas held no interest; it was only his love for my grandmother that allowed him to bear them at all. What he saw in his wife's fascination with revolutionary change was something akin to his own passion for financial adventurism. In their own way, both were looking for the absolute. A quiet life, without fire, without plans, without struggle, was anathema to them. That's why Grandfather was so in love with Grandmother. When she said "revolution," he heard "passion," and felt as though he'd never been closer to anyone. The spirit she brought to her undertaking mattered more to his besotted eyes than did the substance of her enterprise. Her enthusiasm for the Communist revolution—and her conviction—outweighed his lack of interest in the cause; he let her have her way, and he felt happy. Yet Grandfather never allowed money to cut him off from the plight of those less fortunate than he. Indeed, he gave so generously to the poor that he often teased his wife by saying that he did more for social justice today than communism could ever do tomorrow. He also sent a lot of money to his in-laws, who would otherwise have struggled on in crushing poverty.

Grandfather's social and economic star was continually on the rise. When the Second World War broke out, he abandoned the novelty jewelry business for the more lucrative rice trade. Later he opened up a gaming room across from the Kyoto train station, an inspired idea that met with instant success. So great were the profits that Grandfather soon opened up a second casino, then a third, all of which continued to draw great crowds.

The number of Korean immigrants in Japan grew tremendously during the war. Within a few years, their numbers had swelled to 2 million. In addition to those who had come earlier, like my grandparents, hundreds of thousands of men and women were brought over during the war—often forcibly—to help offset labor shortages. Following the end of hostilities, many Koreans stayed on, but the exile community was deeply divided: one part supported the Soviet-backed North Korean administration, the other the American-backed administration in the South. With the outbreak of the Korean War in 1950, emotions flared higher. Positions hardened. The Korean residents formed two ideologically rival associations. The one that favored South Korea called itself *Mindan*, the Democratic Association, while the association that supported the North took the name it still holds today, *Chosen Soren* (Japanese) or *Chochongryon* (Korean), the Federation of Korean Residents in Japan. The latter group held more sway among the exile community; not only was the South having trouble getting its economic motor started, its government had taken in many well-known reactionary errants and given refuge to former pro-Japanese collaborators. The North, by contrast, was posting consistent economic growth and demonstrating unwavering national loyalty.

My grandparents had no idea that North Korea's leadership, like that of Europe's popular democracies, had fallen under Moscow's control and that the Communist leaders who once fought against foreign occupation were being systematically eliminated. Nor did they know that fabricated statistics made North Korea's barely passable economy look like a magnificent success.

Grandfather followed his wife and the rest of the Korean Communists and joined the Chosen Soren, under whose banner were assembled the majority of the poorest Korean emigrants. My grandfather was a decidedly odd case. His massive fortune counted little compared to the influence of his powerful wife. Though not insensitive to the patriotism of his Chosen Soren comrades, what truly mattered to him was joining in my grandmother's feverish activity. While continuing his private businesses, he agreed to direct the association's economic department and even contribute money to it. The growth of Chosen Soren's Kyoto branch, I learned, had a lot to do with his direct financial support.

In June 1949, the Koreans who previously had belonged to the Japanese Communist Party migrated en masse into the newly created Korean Worker's Party, as the North Korean communist party was called. Like its counterparts all over the world, the KWP showed a formidable knack for creating associations with the allure of democracy and openness to the general public. There were women's associations, movements for the defense of culture and peace, sports clubs, and various other groups which the Party could influence from the shadows. My grandmother was among the Party's most active organizers and eventually became director for the Kyoto region. This responsibility came as a supplement to her ordinary commitments as a party member. Had it been humanly possible, I'm sure her relentless activism would have driven her to join even more associations.

Yet she somehow still found time to take charge of her children's upbringing, which she did in a manner all her own. During their years in Kyoto, my grandparents lived in an opulent house located in a picturesque, well-to-do neighborhood dotted with vestiges of

Japan's historic past. The children had their own rooms. The kitchen, or rather kitchens, for there were more than one, were enormous, and paradox of paradoxes, their servants were Japanese—at a time when most domestic workers in Japan were Korean. These luxuries had my grandfather's hand written all over them. Nothing frightened my grandmother more than the effect such comforts might have on her and her family. Was anything more noxious to one's sense of justice than needless luxury? Were not her days in desperate poverty responsible for her understanding of the world? And what a demonstration of the Communist dialectic it had been: the negative turned positive, black misery sublimated into heightened consciousness, suffering into solidarity! "Luxury," she once told me in reference to that period in her life, "is never a leaven to the desire for justice."

And so Grandmother raised her kids as though they were poor. My father told me that he and his siblings often wore darned socks and threadbare clothes, even though their parents had enough money to buy them a new wardrobe several times over. Another anecdote confirms that the kids didn't look like daddy's boys and girls. A rather comic scene took place when, following Japanese custom, my father's teacher was supposed to drop by the house for a parent-teacher conference. Since the teacher had never visited before, my father led the way. The closer they got to the house, the more astonished and incredulous the teacher became. "You must be lost," said the teacher. "We're going toward the rich neighborhood." "No, no," retorted my father. "It's just around the corner." The teacher continued to voice his astonishment, but there was no mistake, and the bewildered man soon found himself standing inside a beautiful house in Kyoto's poshest neighborhood. I later saw the house in a home movie my father had shot and brought with him to the North. It was a luxurious three-story villa with a pool and a garden.

I have always been at a loss to understand why my grandparents sent their kids to ordinary Japanese schools rather than institutions run by the Chosen Soren. These bastions of the counterculture were favored by parents who wanted their children tapped into their Korean roots. Why my father, uncles, and aunts never attended these schools will forever remain a mystery.

The Chosen Soren education network remained strong throughout the 1960s and 1970s and comprised some 150 institutions spanning primary school to university. By the 1980s, however, the network had been substantially weakened by the integration of Japan's 700,000 Korean residents into the mainstream culture, as well as by North Korea's withering public image and the general lack of interest in becoming "a proud soldier of General Kim Il-sung."

Though it has lost much of its power and glory, the Chosen Soren still exists. In May 1998, it held its eighteenth congress and reelected to its head the stalwart old leader Han Duk-su (of whom more later). The Chosen Soren still owns a few dozen companies and controls some fifteen news organizations. Their profits help buttress North Korea's economy much the way money from Miami's exile community helps to sustain Cuba. In 1998, nearly $80 million was reportedly transferred from Japan to North Korea.

After completing high school, my father enrolled at the University of Kyoto to pursue his great artistic passion for photography—despite being slated, as the eldest son, to replace his father in the family's thriving casino business. The other children were excellent students who seemed destined for great success. My first aunt was a pharmacist; my first uncle, who attended the Waseida University of Tokyo, was a journalist; and the other siblings studied medicine and biology.

The leaders of the Chosen Soren were very keen on seeing people with advanced education return to North Korea, and they continually played up the homeland's need for individuals with knowledge and abilities. In North Korea a person could serve the people and the state rather than Japan, that pawn of American imperialism. Yet the Chosen Soren did not limit itself to recruiting the Korean elite, but worked tirelessly for the repatriation of every class of Korean emigrant. The true mastermind behind the Chosen Soren's campaign was the North Korean state. In the 1960s, under Kim Il-sung's direction, it made enormous efforts to lure Korean emigrants by representing itself as the last hope for reunification and the defense of national identity: for South Korea was reactionary and a puppet of the United States.

Koreans never had an easy time integrating into Japanese life and often were targets of prejudice. The North Korean propaganda thus resonated with many in the diaspora, and thousands responded to Kim Il-sung's call to return. Well-to-do Koreans such as my grandparents could expect to be wooed with an equal measure of ideological arguments and fantastical promises: there were managerial positions awaiting them, they were entitled to a beautiful home, they would have no material worries, and their children would be able to study in Moscow. Grandfather was rather against the idea, Grandmother all for it. Interminable conversations followed, from which my grandmother ultimately emerged victorious. No one was particularly surprised. And so it was that the family found itself heading for North Korea.

THREE

NEXT YEAR IN
PYONGYANG!

Grandfather agreed to the move, but he continued to drag his feet. The circumstances under which he ultimately arrived at his decision are rather comical, especially considering the political and economic stakes. Sometime in the past, Grandfather had become fast friends with the head *yakusa*, or boss, of the Kyoto mob. My grandfather was utterly enthralled by him and believed him to possess extraordinary intelligence, business acumen, courage, and, in a certain sense, honesty. My grandfather's confidence in him was boundless. He and the *yakusa* were more than friends; they were like brothers, by which I infer they once took an oath of friendship. It is a common practice in the Far East, where two people become bound through an exchange of letters or of blood. What Europeans might consider a game for children is serious business for adults in that part of the world, and I'm sure that Grandfather and the local mafia boss truly considered theirs an oath for life. When time came

21

for Grandfather to make up his mind, he naturally sought out this man's advice, and it was this gangster who dispelled his last lingering doubts by telling him it was his duty to respond to the call of the fatherland, to help it flourish, and to change his life.

Thus was determined the fate of my family, and mine with it. Everyone—those, such as my Grandmother, who really wanted to leave and those, such as my father and most of his siblings, who were merely resigned to leaving—boarded the ship for Korea. Even my first uncle, who was dead set against moving, couldn't get out of it. Some members of the extended family tried to rally behind him, and certain cousins even offered to take him in. He put up a good fight, but winning ultimately would have entailed breaking with his parents, something he was not ready to do. He tried to explain his reasons for wanting to stay and even offered to manage the family casinos while continuing his university studies. Grandfather refused: once resolved to leave, he wanted to make a clean break of it. For my uncle the idea of leaving the country where he had grown up and gone to school, where his parents had met and fallen in love, was unthinkable. At boarding time, he ran away to his cousins' house. Grandmother had to go there and fetch him, and when he refused to obey her—a rare thing in those days—she slapped him and dragged him to the docks, arriving just as the ship was about to sail.

My uncle still had one option remaining: he could raise a protest before the Japanese authorities, claim that his parents were taking him against his will, and request the protection of the Japanese state. When it had come to the Japanese government's attention that the Worker's Party and its associations were pressing heads of households to depart with their entire families, it opened a small government office near the turnstile of the Korean-bound ships, where a bureaucrat and several members of the Red Cross interviewed departing passengers to verify that they were leaving of their own accord.

My uncle wavered until the last moment. A terrible struggle took place inside of him. On one side was his love for his parents and his wish to obey them, on the other, his attachment to his current life and his uncertainty about the life awaiting him abroad. Perhaps he also had some dark foreboding. Still undecided, his eyes crossed his mother's fearsome, imperious gaze, and his choice seemed already made. The authorities asked him if he personally wanted to move to Korea, and he answered that, yes, he did. And there, too, was a destiny sealed.

On the ship over, the long-awaited dream seemed actually to materialize. The family was treated with perfect solicitude, lodged in a luxury cabin and regaled with the finest meals. While the other returning patriots were treated like ordinary passengers, my family was catered to like Communist Party cadres—better yet, like a group headed to honor Kim Il-sung on his birthday. Grandmother told me that one of the ship's passengers was Kim Yong-ghil, a Korean opera singer who had found fame and fortune in Japan. As the ship approached the Korean coast, he got up on the bridge, turned to the promised land, and sang "O Sole Mio," causing emotions to swell among the passengers standing within earshot. The poor man. He was an artist who wanted to share his gifts with the people, but he wound up being condemned as a spy and sent to die in the Senghori hard-labor camp—reputedly one of North Korea's harshest. When he first arrived in North Korea the regime welcomed him with great pomp, and Kim Il-sung even granted him the honor of a long handshake. In Japan, Kim Yong-ghil has gained legendary stature, having become a symbol of the tragedy undergone by so many Japanese residents who moved to North Korea. Call me hard-hearted, but I think the only thing Kim Yong-ghil symbolizes is foolishness.

His story—which is equally the story of my family and of all those who leapt so confidently into the maw of misfortune—mostly demonstrates the force of human illusion and its awesome power to render us utterly blind. I have since learned that at other latitudes and at other times, the same Communist powers created similar traps for making people believe and hope in illusions. This led to the misery of countless peoples: in France, in America, in Egypt, and perhaps most notably, in Armenia. Tens of thousands died there in 1947 under the spell of Stalin's propaganda, which had painted the Soviet Socialist Republic of Armenia as the land of milk and honey. The Soviets allowed that much remained to be done and that everyone would have to roll up their sleeves, but it also promised that the ancestral culture and religion would be respected and that the newcomers would shortly see a new generation rise and flourish in social justice.

The Koreans who enthusiastically cast off from the port of Nikada on Japan's western coast were like those Armenians who left from the Port of Marseilles fifteen years earlier, tossing loaves of good white bread, that had been distributed to them, to their relatives on shore. Several years later they were cursing themselves and anyone who had ever told them about that land of supposed plenty. They sent desperate appeals to France, were willing to do anything just to get out. But it was too late. It was just the same for the returning Korean patriots. They set off full of confidence and hope, often with Japanese spouses and children who had only known life in Japan, and they, too, were heading for a big fall, at the bottom of which they would find isolation, poverty, daily surveillance, and sometimes, the concentration camps.

At the end of a fifteen-hour voyage, my grandparents landed in Chongjin in northeastern Korea. My third uncle later told me about the family's arrival: "It was like the city was dead—the strangest atmosphere. The people all looked so shabby and aimless in their wandering. There was a feeling of deep sadness in the air, and no movement betrayed the slightest hint of spontaneity." My uncle was frightened by these shadows, who were so at odds with the earthly paradise he had been led to expect. A sense of dull terror lent new weight to the warnings his family had received prior to its departure. But what reason had they to heed the reactionaries' drivel? My uncle downplayed one incident that later came back to him like a boomerang: when the passengers descended down to the docks, several Koreans, who had arrived from Japan a few weeks earlier, took advantage of the general mayhem of family reunions to whisper their astonishment at the new arrivals' decision to immigrate.

One of them came up to my uncle. "What happened?" he asked. "We sent our friends and family letters warning people not to come! Why didn't your family listen?" My uncle turned suddenly pale. My father stepped forward and answered in his place, asking the young man how long he'd been in the North. "A few months," he answered, "but that's long enough to understand." My father insisted that the Chosen Soren had hidden nothing of the difficulties and challenges involved in building the country. "But it's just propaganda," responded his interlocutor. "You're not going to build a new life here; your parents will be stripped of all their belongings, then left to die. You'll soon find out what these North Korean Communists are all about."

The furtive exchange cast a palpable chill. This wasn't the sort of welcome my father and uncle had expected. Yet it was true that these detractors had only recently arrived. Big moves always take some adjustment; these people just hadn't been there long enough.

And why had that strange man come up to them afterward? Might they not have been provocateurs? Grandmother later pointed out that if their intention really was to get us to turn back, they certainly picked the wrong time and place to do it. "We were wearing rose-colored glasses when we arrived. Our faith in our new life was anchored so deep, had been cultivated for so long, that these grim warnings simply couldn't touch us." Besides that, it looked like the North Korea dream might still prove a reality: the receiving officials waited on the family hand and foot. While the other newly arriving immigrants were summarily routed off to various cities around the country, my family received the sort of attention generally reserved for Party cadres. Grandfather had brought his car over on the ship. It was a late model Volvo—probably the only one of its kind in all North Korea. The officials suggested the family drive the Volvo to Pyongyang while a second, government, car followed with the family's luggage. The authorities trusted them and tried to make their arrival as pleasant and agreeable as possible.

The family spent their first few weeks in a shabby temporary apartment before being moved, as promised, into a beautiful new house in the capital, not far from the central train station and very close to the Soviet embassy. Despite the relative prosperity of Pyongyang and the magnificence of the countryside, despite Pyongyang's cleanliness and the majesty of its monuments, a feeling of malaise soon set in. With every passing day, the family felt more forgotten. There were no official visits, no warm welcomes from the new neighbors, no updates from the central bureaucracy, which claimed always to be awaiting further instructions from on high.

They were a long way from the brotherly relations advertised by the propagandists in Kyoto; a long way, too, from the collective effort the country needed—the effort that was supposed to be paved with difficulties and sacrifices but also with enthusiasm and brotherhood. The family felt like it was missing some of the pieces it needed to make sense of the situation, but no one was eager to help fill in the blanks. I'm sure it wasn't long before they began fearing they had made a mistake. Their apprehensions could only deepen before the ubiquitous propaganda, the food shortages, and the incompetence of an ultra-hierarchical bureaucracy incapable of addressing even the most basic problems of everyday life: how to get food, how to find an electrician, a hairdresser, a doctor. Why was it so difficult to get eight gallons of gas? Why were the neighborhood's Party representatives nowhere to be found? Why was the family left with nothing to do when it wanted to make itself useful? Nothing corresponded to their expectations. Among the children, none wanted to be the first to confess the feeling they all shared: the feeling that maybe, just maybe, their parents had led them down a bad road.

Since everyone was being kept waiting—the children for their admittance to the university and my grandparents for their prospective jobs—Grandfather decided the family should get to know the country a bit better. Making the best of a difficult situation, he took the whole family out for long meandering drives in the Volvo. It was during these vacations that the family first felt the grip of government surveillance. They didn't get far before members of the People's Security Force, the political police, let my grandfather understand that in North Korea outings were not undertaken without authorization. My grandfather and uncles were indignant at the admonition, which they saw as a manifestation of the country's idiotic bureaucracy.

At long last my grandmother was summoned to appear before officials of the Union of Korean Democratic Women, an association that the Worker's Party controlled every bit as tightly as it did the Chosen Soren. Grandmother was awarded the vice-presidency of the association's Pyongyang section. Later she was also elected deputy to the People's Supreme Assembly, a purely honorific position which nevertheless made her very proud, as did the three medals the government subsequently awarded her. Grandfather's appointment, when it finally came, was also to his liking. He was named vice-president of the Office for the Management of Commercial Affairs, the agency responsible, among other things, for managing the flow of foodstuffs into the capital. It was this position that accounted for our surfeit of select foods and the frequent honorific visits by interested officials.

My mother was also born to a family of Koreans residing in Japan. My maternal grandfather, a native of the southern city of Taegu, had worked as an undercover operative of the Pyongyang regime. One day he was arrested by the Japanese police and died in custody. The North Korean government subsequently named him an official hero of the revolution and awarded his survivors the title of heroic family. Who would not wish to return to a country where one's husband was a hero? My maternal grandmother, her five daughters in tow, thus left Japan without a moment's hesitation, arriving in North Korea shortly after my paternal grandparents. The six women settled in Nampo, a large port city on the western coast. While the rest of the family stayed in Nampo, my mother and her youngest sister moved to Pyongyang to study economics and medicine, respectively. All five sisters were soon married off through the agency of a matchmaker, as was customary at the time. Still today, a fourth of the marriages in South Korea and half of those in supposedly revolutionary North Korea are arranged with little, if any, consultation with the spouses-to-be. This was how my mother and father met and married in 1967.

By the time I was born, my family—by that I mean the part of the family that lived under the same roof: my paternal grandparents, my mother and father, and my third uncle—had grown accustomed to life in North Korea. It had more than its share of daily dissatisfactions, but thanks to my grandparents' jobs and the packages that kept arriving from friends and family back in Japan, it was not without its material comforts. Friends and playmates always wanted to come to my house, because they knew they would get cold cuts, sweets, and desserts. Yet my grandfather's position was also the cause of constant worry, and it eventually cost him his life. He was a businessman who had learned how to get things done under a free market system. When faced with the muddle of North Korean bureaucracy, he tended to let his frustration show, which in retrospect was not too wise. Though he only ever criticized the country's excellent political and economic methods "for the sake of improving and strengthening the country," his desire for reform inevitably collided with his "comrades'" lapidary work routines. He had constantly to endure their animosity, which since he refused to keep quiet, only grew. Despite all the honors and benefits that sprang from my grandparents' positions, North Korean life was not meeting the family's expectations. The ideological shackles foisted on every North Korean, the sometimes discreet, sometimes indiscreet police surveillance weighed heavily on the children. They judged severely the poverty of this would-be paradise and the narrowness of its intellectual and artistic life. Eventually, something inside them gave way and the long-restrained accusations began to fly. "Why did you bring us here? You promised us we would have a new life. We've lost our freedom. We don't even have the bare essentials you can find anywhere in Japan. We're not happy here. And neither are you, only you don't want to admit it."

My grandparents were embarrassed, flustered. I think Grandfather was the first to realize he'd been had. The head of our family, whose stature alone was once enough to quell any thought of rebellion, looked everyday more defeated, was everyday less like the man his children had once dubbed "tiger face." Gone was that sense of haughty self-assurance and, along with it, his sons' fear of speaking their minds. Grandmother, on the other hand, pretending to still hope for an improvement in the situation, stalwartly countered the criticisms indirectly aimed at Kim Il-sung. Communist ideology had supplied her with an inexhaustible supply of ready-made retorts, which she never hesitated to unleash upon her children: "What impatience! How can you expect a country to be rich a mere ten years after the terrible destruction wrought by the imperialist Americans? Everything needs to be rebuilt from the ground up. Have you forgotten that enemies still walk in the corridors of power? How can the dictatorship of the proletariat possibly loosen its grip? Have you no confidence in the awesome leader we are so privileged to follow?" Her kids shrugged their shoulders. They felt North Korea had received them not as compatriots but as foreigners—worse, as foreigners who were responsible for being so. The North Korean state was eager to collect the Japanese residents' money, but it made no effort to dispel the mistrust many natives felt toward the newly arrived.

While the atmosphere never prevented my aunts and uncles from advancing brilliantly in their studies, there was no longer any mention of the prospect, once dangled before them, of going to Moscow. My first uncle became a journalist after studying philosophy at Kim Il-sung University; my second uncle earned his degree in gastroenterology from the department of medicine in Pyongyang; and my third uncle became a biologist after majoring in natural sciences at the University of Pyongsan. As for my aunts, one studied pharmacology, then did research for a pharmaceutical factory in Pyongyang. My second aunt studied medicine, then married a young man whose family—also emigrated from Japan—had recently been sent to the camps. When my grandmother learned of the deportation, she acted quickly to try to extricate her daughter from this reactionary milieu. Since her daughter was pregnant, she urged her to get an abortion and generally did everything in her power to cause a rift in the marriage. Her efforts were unsuccessful, however, and the couple stayed together. Later, when it came our turn to be arrested, Grandmother underwent the added humiliation of finding herself face to face with these reactionaries. As for my father, who had studied photography in Japan, he climbed his way to the head of Pyongyang's biggest studio, the Ongnyu—or "Clear Water"—Photo Shop. As a semiofficial state photographer, he spent much of his time shooting public ceremonies and printing portraits of Party leaders.

All this might be thought an indication of the family's integration and success, but that's not the way it felt. The family's bitterness ran deep. My father and his siblings knew that, even if they wanted to, their parents couldn't officially request to return to Japan. Doing so could even be dangerous. Their unhappy decision to move to North Korea was irreversible, and they all thought of themselves as prisoners. At a certain point, my first uncle stopped raising the issue with his parents. That big man, who was once so outgoing and full of life, became more taciturn and morose by the day. My second uncle, who was more interested in comic books than official literature, began to drink heavily—another manner of expressing oneself without saying a word. Only my third uncle managed to keep his spirits high. His passion for botany and biology were strong enough to make him overlook political reality. He collected plants and insects, and his display boards were even catalogued in the museum. It's ironic that he was the only one of my uncles to be sent to the camps. Unlike his two brothers, who had married and moved out of the house, he continued to live with his parents, and so suffered the family's fate.

Growing up, I was never aware of my uncles' disaffection with Kim Il-sung: I was too young to imagine such a thing was possible. Looking back now, their transformation seems telling: the silence of one, the alcoholism of the other, my father's sudden obsession with music. They were each running away from reality, avoiding the words that might indict the political system or, worse yet, the parents who had brought them to live in it. My father was learning all the popular international songs by heart. He knew "Nathalie" and "La Paloma." To our great joy, he also sang us the famous "O Sole Mio." I now realize this was his way of escaping the military marching music and the glory hymns to Kim Il-sung.

I mentioned that he had been married to a woman whose family also had returned from Japan. Many marriages took place within this immigrant community, which proves just how difficult integrating into Korean society really was. The former Japanese residents, especially the young ones, had grown up in a different culture. This made communication with North Koreans difficult. Neighbors and security agents never let slip an opportunity to remind them that they were no longer in Japan, that they should express less originality, that they should show more respect for the laws.

Having been exposed to the wider world, my parents, like most former Japanese residents, felt superior to the people who never left

North Korea. Their payback was being viewed as strangers. The old enmity between Korea and Japan also played against us. To many people, my family's former immigration to Japan seemed more important than its decision to come back. The family's material advantages were also the cause of barely veiled jealousy. As part of the next generation, I always felt profoundly and unequivocally Korean—indeed, North Korean. Yet, even as a young child, I sensed the chasm that separated my parents from their neighbors. My mother's accent, which bore traces of her years in Japan, was the cause of constant laughter among my friends. Every time she got home from work and called me back inside, they would mimic her voice, making me blush with embarrassment. Finally I asked her not to do it anymore. I think I hurt her feelings, but she didn't say anything, and from then on, whenever she wanted me to come home, she walked over to where I was playing and gave me a little tap on the shoulder.

To put it simply, the repatriated Koreans didn't get on with the others, just as the Armenians from France and America didn't fit in with their Soviet kinsmen. Though growing sulkier by the day, Grandfather did rattle the chains occasionally. Supplied with the necessary paperwork, he sometimes got out the Volvo and took us on trips around the countryside. That's how we wound up visiting the famous tourist destination of Mount Kumgang, lately in the news because of tour groups brought there by a South Korean travel company, Hyndai, which pays the Pyongyang government millions of dollars in royalties. At the time, driving to Mount Kumgang in a car so emblematic of capitalist ostentation might have been seen as a provocation. We were verging on counterrevolutionary action! Yet the police seemed not to notice and gave us what authorizations we needed without much hassle, a solicitude due at least in part to the generous sums my grandfather dispersed among the Security Force and the state.

Later the authorizations became more difficult to come by. Then the police began suggesting my grandfather should voluntarily bequeath his cherished Volvo to the government. The suggestions became recommendations, the recommendations an order. At last my grandfather had to cede his Volvo, most likely to some well-placed police or government official who wanted a nice car in which to strut about town. As the family's situation worsened, Japan became an ever-expanding reservoir of idealized memories, nostalgic images, favorable dispositions. My family was once again a family of uprooted emigrants. That feeling of nostalgia is still in the family, but with every generation its object continues to shift. My grandfather lived in Japan full of longing for his native Cheju Island. My father lived in North Korea and was nostalgic for Japan. And me, I sit recalling my life's story in Seoul, gnawed at by the Pyongyang of my youth.

FOUR

In a Concentration Camp at the Age of Nine

Though even more anxious and withdrawn, Grandfather remained the central character of the family. His pronounced eyebrows, round, sparkling eyes, and stentorian voice always enthralled me. So, too, did the respect shown him by Pyongyang's Party cadres. And yet this never got in the way of our intimacy. Our Sunday walks, in tones of high secrecy, he would tell me stories about his former days in Kyoto: about the jewelry shop where he stayed up all night filling his first orders, the rice warehouses he guarded against envious competitors, the stunning success of his gaming rooms; and the fortunes that grew and fell there in a matter of minutes. These stories were a source of constant enchantment for me. I listened, mesmerized, to their architect and hero, my grandfather. I loved him, and never could I have imagined that our conversations and Sunday walks might one day come to an end.

Yet he disappeared. It was in July of 1977. One night he didn't come home from work. The police said they knew nothing. The heads of my grandfather's department, whom my grandmother anxiously queried, finally told us he had left on a business trip, an urgent matter, they said. The order had come from the Party, and he had to decide right away. "But come back next week and you'll have some news," they assured her. "There's no need to worry."

My grandmother had her doubts about this business trip. Her husband was not the type to leave without warning. A week later, the authorities told her to keep waiting, but she was unable to restrain herself and went back to my grandfather's office. The reception she met with only deepened her fears. Everyone seemed embarrassed by the mere mention of her husband's name and avoided talking about him. The same wall of nervous silence soon cropped up everywhere Grandmother went.

My parents suspected that the Security Force was behind the mysterious disappearance, but they dared not admit this even to themselves. In the preceding months a number of their acquaintances had vanished in similar ways. Yet the family preferred to believe—my grandmother more than anyone—that there was no comparison between my grandfather and those others, who must have plotted against the state or committed some other grave offense. None of us was willing to face the possibility that the police had taken him away from us. We knew that Grandfather was never at a loss for words and that he often criticized Party bureaucrats and their management methods rather too sharply. We also knew that he rarely showed up at Party meetings and rallies, but then again, Grandmother attended enough for two! And had he not always been an honest citizen, entrusting his all to the Party? Had he not handed over his immense fortune upon arriving from Japan? Had he not given the Party every-thing, down to his Volvo?

A few weeks after Grandfather's disappearance, I was playing on the riverbank when several of my friends came to tell me that a group of people were at my house. Puzzled, I got up and ran to our apartment.

Traditionally, people take their shoes off on entering a Korean home. Not doing so is a sign of disrespect to your host. To my aston-ishment, I noticed that though the living room was full of people, the entrance hall had only the usual number of shoes. What did this mean? I wanted to move forward, but there were so many people in the room it was hard to maneuver. Apart from my father, mother, grandmother, and sister, there were a number of other people whom I had never seen before. The only one missing was my uncle, who lived with us but was away for a few days at a professional confer-ence in south Hamkyung Province. Who were these other people? I greeted my parents with a big wave, but they, who were ordinarily so happy to see me, responded strangely, remaining distant, like con-descending adults who hadn't time for such trifles. My mother sighed and kept on repeating (as though someone would answer!), "But what is happening to us? But what is happening to us?" I pushed forward, determined to see what was going on: three uni-formed men were rifling through our things as a fourth took notes. What extraordinary event was this? And how could they keep their shoes on? That was what shocked me the most, but when I tried to tell my mother, she didn't even answer me.

Our apartment consisted of four bedrooms and a living room. The smallest bedroom stored wrapped gifts my grandparents had requested from friends and family who had visited from Japan over the years. The cache of jewelry, clothes, and watches was to be presented at the wedding of my third uncle—whenever that was going to be. (It is customary for Korean families to begin preparing for their children's wedding far—often years—in advance.) The room also contained several cameras and various darkroom materials that my father used in his work. These treasures greatly excited the security agents—for these were who our four visitors were. In the past, my parents had been "encouraged" to offer one of the cameras as a gift to the state but had always found a pretext for refusing. This time the agents were simply going to help themselves. My father later told me about the agents' secret councils in the corner of the room, about their mock indignation at finding the wedding gifts—as though we were smugglers or harborers of stolen goods— and about the spark of covetousness and joy in their eyes as they divvied up the loot in plain view of my distraught parents.

The agents then pressed on through the rest of the apartment, three searching, while the fourth continued to take notes. The inventory progressed slowly, and I soon grew bored of a situation that didn't really involve me, since the gentlemen seemed not the least interested in my aquariums. I went and got my sister, Mi-ho, and we started to play, indifferent to what might come next. We were soon running around, romping in the shambles left by the search. I started to jump up and down on my parents' big Japanese bed and encouraged my sister to do the same. My father noticed but made no attempt to stop this ordinarily forbidden game. Heartened, I jumped ever higher, until what was bound to happen, happened: I broke a mattress spring, or a lattice, I no longer remember which. My sister and I froze. A boundary had been crossed, we knew that. And yet Father still said nothing. I don't know what my sister thought of that paternal abdication, but it left me feeling very strange. The order of things had changed. I was not yet worried, but I began to feel a certain malaise, the shape and cause of which I could not altogether comprehend. Perhaps this is why a hole persists there in my memory.

Yet I remember perfectly the moment I first heard pronounced the name of "Yodok." One of the agents had begun rifling through my mother's lingerie, and seeing her private things tossed across the room, my mother allowed her voice to rise. Outraged, the man with the notebook jumped to his feet, ordering her to shut up, then pulled out a paper from which he read out loud. According to the document, my grandfather had committed "a crime of high treason," the consequence of which was that his family—all of us there gathered, that is—was "immediately" to present itself at the secure zone in Yodok, a canton of which I had never heard. Everyone around me seemed to go dead. There was a long silence, then tears, and hands taking hold of one another. Clearly reaping pleasure from the effect of his words, the leader ordered his men to resume their work. The agents turned the place inside out, going through the bedding, the clothes, the mattresses, the kitchen utensils. I looked on bewildered, unable to understand what they could be looking for among the bowls and the plates and the pots and even my chest of toys. The inventory wound to a close around three in the morning. The agents performed their work according to well-defined rules— of their own invention—with a small cut going to the government, and a bigger cut going to them. My father's photo equipment and Omega wristwatch, my mother's and grandmother's jewelry, my uncle's wedding presents, and the family's Japanese color television set were all shared among the agents. No more than one item out of ten was left to the government.

There is one moment that particularly stands out in my memory of that night. My grandmother was having a face-off with the agents. They were trying to force her to sign a document, but she objected, pointing insistently at certain passages. The agents offered some perfunctory explanations, their tone alternating between calm restraint and outbursts of angry shouting. Suddenly I saw her reach for the pen holder and sign the paper. The next thing that happened surprised me even more: she had hardly finished signing when the men grabbed her and locked her up in one of the rooms!

When sunrise came and I learned we'd soon be leaving for that unknown place whose mention had so jolted my parents, I was not overly upset. I thought of it as a move to the country, an adventure, something to bring a little excitement to our lives. Truth be told, the idea actually pleased me. My one real concern was finding a way to bring my fish collection along. In some respects, our departure for Yodok resembled a move. We weren't being sent to the camps as criminals but as relatives of a criminal, which meant we were treated with a little more clemency. My grandfather had been picked up from work and taken away to a hard-labor camp without even the chance to pack a bag. His fate was like that of many people arrested in the USSR and Nazi Germany, whose history I was later able to read. We, at least, were allowed to bring a minimum of furniture, clothes, and even food.

From a certain perspective, our case could be seen as one of simple banishment, but as we would soon discover, the barbed wire, the huts, the malnutrition, and the mind-quashing work left little doubt that it really was a concentration camp. The camp's policy of maintaining the cohesion of the family unit merely testifies to the resilience—even in a supposedly Communist country—of the

Confucian tradition. This policy does not, however, alter the basic nature of the camp. The stated purpose of sending us away as a family was to reeducate us through work and study. As noncriminals who were contaminated by the reactionary ideology of the criminal in our midst, we were ordered to a place built specifically for the "redeemable" cases. But I'm getting ahead of myself.

The search completed, my parents began packing with the help of several employees from my grandfather's office. They had arrived early in the morning, conscripted, perhaps, by the security agents looking to hasten our departure. My grandfather's former colleagues might have been pleased to lend my family a helping hand, but it is unlikely that the gesture was a spontaneous one. Showing solidarity with a criminal family was dangerous. Indeed, since the arrival of security only one person had dared drop in for a visit. That one exception was an old lady who lived on our floor. She knocked on our door, then slipped her slight little figure in among the packing boxes. She smiled at everyone, greeted the agents politely, and generally did her best to blend into the wallpaper. She then glided over to my grandmother and whispered in her ear. "Be strong, dear. Have courage. . . . Don't ever give up. You have no reason to blame yourself, and you know your husband did nothing wrong. And a final bit of advice: when you're in a difficult spot, think about your children and your grandchildren and you'll make it."

As our bundles were being loaded into the five large crates allotted us, I saw my sister take hold of her favorite doll. This gave me an idea: I hurriedly grabbed one of my aquariums and stocked it with a selection of my most beautiful fish. I then hugged the aquarium fast against me, just as I saw my sister do with her doll. One of the agents noticed me and said that taking "that"—gesturing to the aquarium with his chin—was out of the question. The brutality of the order, handed down by someone I didn't even know, threw me into a raging fit. I ranted and raved, yelled and bawled so much the agent finally relented. My swell of tears gradually abated, but the fate of the fish left behind still worried me. When I was first told of the strange goings-on at my house, several of my more treacherous friends said I would probably be sent to "a nasty place" and so would do well to give my fish away to my pals. At the time I hadn't taken their offer seriously, but now, on the cusp of my departure, I regretted it.

A truck was stationed in front our building. The men began loading the crates and the few small furnishings the agents didn't want for themselves: a low table, some kitchen utensils, and a 125-pound bag of rice, the maximum the camp would allow. The rattle of the engine, the lamentations of some, and the orders of others began waking the neighbors. One by one, lights came on in the surrounding apartments. I could see people staring from behind their windowpanes. Some worked up the courage to come down for a closer look. The gathering crowd kept a reserved distance, but it wasn't the sort of assembly the agents liked much, and they now did their best to move everything along more quickly. A minor panic ensued when my father bolted back to the apartment to fetch a few last-minute things. That reminded me of my favorite comic books. Like all the kids, I loved the story about the battle of the hedgehog army, in which the hedgehogs and squirrels join forces to defeat the wolves, rats, foxes, and eagles, all representative of the horrible world of capitalism. I begged the security agent—I think he was the same one who had given way to my earlier temper tantrum—to let me go get it. But by now he'd had enough of my antics and screamed for me to get in the truck. This time I was scared and obeyed without protest. So much for the hedgehog army. At least I had my favorite fish.

My family climbed one by one into the back of the truck, except for my mother, who, to my great surprise, remained standing on the sidewalk. I still remember the immense sadness in her face, streaming with tears. "You're not coming?" I asked. "No, not right away, my love. I'll join you soon." In a hurry to wrap things up, the agents brusquely confirmed my mother's words and kept everyone going about their business. Reassured, I squeezed myself up against my aquarium, which I topped with a plank of wood to keep the water from sloshing out. After a final good-bye, my attention turned to the novelty of riding in an automobile, a rare event in the life of a private North Korean citizen.

My poor mother! It must have been terrible for her. Much as she tried, she couldn't hide her sadness. Yet her little nine-year-old son had understood almost nothing. He had climbed into the truck quite happily, his fish pressed to his chest. His mother didn't know so many years would pass before she would see her son again. The daughter of a "heroic family," she was spared a trip to the camp where her children and husband spent the next ten years. Shortly after our imprisonment, the Security Force made her get a divorce and terminate all ties with our family of "traitors." She was never asked her opinion, never even gave her signature. She suffered greatly and longed for her lost family throughout the long years of our imprisonment. I later learned she had repeatedly appealed to the Security Force for permission to join us in the camp, but her requests were seen as aberrant and never granted.

We started out just as the day was breaking. The truck was a Tsir, the powerful Soviet-built machine that was standard equipment for hauling away prisoners. The Koreans called it "the crow," a symbol of death, for though white remains the traditional color of mourning in Korea, black is the color of funerals. It was a covered truck, and during the first leg of the trip, my sister and I were not allowed to peek outside. Once we were out in the country, however, the agents let us watch at the passing scenery as much as we wanted. The ride was bumpy, traversing rutted, packed-earth roads. I was holding up fine myself—my one real concern was keeping the water from sloshing out of the aquarium—but Mi-ho started vomiting. Grandmother found her a plastic bag, then spread blankets on the truck floor for her to lie on. Our crates and furnishings were in the forward part of the bed. Two armed security agents stood guarding the back.

At one point my grandmother asked the agents what they intended to do with her youngest son, the one absent member of the household. She said he was innocent and that they had no reason to arrest him. The agents agreed. Now that I think of it, Grandmother must have been pretty desperate. She must have known the guards were powerless to decide anything. All she was looking for was a little consolation, and in some way, perhaps she found it. Yet when our questions turned to the place we were being taken to, the guards claimed ignorance. They did try to cheer us up, though, and even showed a little benevolence, but they swore up and down they didn't even know what a camp looked like. "All I know," said one of them, "is that it's not too bad a place. Nothing's going to happen to you."

Keeping us calm was apparently the guards' main responsibility. It was common knowledge that people in our situation often preferred to take their own lives. The guards wanted none of that. Suicide was a manner of disobeying, of showing that one had lost faith in the future traced out by the Party. The soldiers' good cheer was intended to preserve the utopian myth long enough to get us to our destination. But it did little to stanch my grandmother's crying or to keep my father from sinking into morose silence. Was he thinking about his wife? Remembering the house in Kyoto? His happier days learning photography with his friends? Grandmother's unshakeable desire to leave Japan and return to the Fatherland of the Revolution? Everything had gone from bad to worse since that decision in which he hardly had a word. The arrest must have seemed to him like the latest in a series of steps on the descent to hell.

He was sitting in front of me, hollow-eyed, lost in thought. A little farther on, the truck came to a stop and one of the agents jumped out. A minute later he was back, escorting an elderly woman around my grandmother's age. She was well dressed, all in black, without luggage. We all figured she was an acquaintance or relative of the guard, hitching a ride. She was silent at first, but after about fifteen minutes she started talking and then never stopped. It turned out she, too, was on her way to Yodok, her story running parallel to our own—from her decision to emigrate from Kyoto to the precursory disappearance of her husband, accused of espionage. She had no children and was now entirely on her own, unable to understand why she was being taken away. When she started criticizing the Party, the two agents, who had been standing silently by, ordered her to shut up. But she continued, only less loudly, and the guards, whose only concern was avoiding problems, pretended not to hear.

"How will I survive there without children or a husband?" she kept asking.

"If we're sent to the same camp, you can count on us: we'll stick together," responded my grandmother.

The woman thanked her, her nerves a little soothed. She'd packed twenty hard-boiled eggs for the journey and now began handing them out to everyone in the truck, including the security agents. When I got my egg, I crumbled up the yoke to feed it to my fish. But as I prepared to sprinkle the yellow crumbs onto the surface of the aquarium, my grandmother slapped me hard across the face and ordered me to eat. It was the first time she had ever raised her hand against me. I was devastated but did as I was told, eating the powdered yoke I had designated for my beloved fish. The hours passed slowly. When I grew bored, I climbed up on the crates and looked out through a little Plexiglas window. But most of the time I stayed seated, stunned by the memory of that slap and grieving the death of several of my fish. I wanted terribly to cry but fought back tears with all my strength. I covered the aquarium again and held it tightly in my arms, looking straight ahead, forcing myself to think of nothing. The dirt road continued to climb through twists and hairpin turns. The old strategic route, originally built by the Japanese to connect the eastern and western parts of North Korea, was known to be extremely dangerous. With all the bumps and turns, I, too, lost my stomach. Finally, toward midday we reached Wolwangnyong, the King's Pass, 3,000 feet above tree line. North Koreans also call it the Pass of Tears, because it's the last stretch of road on the way to Yodok. It was two o'clock before we arrived at the perimeter of the camp. When the truck came to a halt, none of the adults wanted to look outside. Over the last several hours they'd had plenty of opportunity to get used to the landscape, but Lord only knew what they would see if they looked out now. They didn't move, so I didn't move either, and we all just sat there, waiting for something to happen.

다섯

FIVE

WORK GROUP
NUMBER 10

The two security agents climbed down from the back of the truck. Outside, I could hear them whispering to other people. In a moment, one of the guards returned and asked for the passports of the adults and the birth certificates of the children. He took the documents and disappeared. Twenty minutes passed under heavy silence, then the guards returned. They climbed back into the truck and we slowly set off again. Curiosity was getting the better of me, and encountering no objection from the guards, I climbed up to look through the peephole.

In front of us, soldiers were swinging open a gate. On the archway above it I could make out the words, "Border Patrol of the Korean People, Unit 2915." The sign didn't impress me much at the time, but I now realize it was yet another link in the interminable chain of lies, a way of camouflaging the camp to look like an army

barracks, distracting the attention of the outside world. A crude lie
it was, considering how far Yodok is from the border. The gateway
was the only opening in a long concrete wall. Above it rose two
watchtowers. Farther off, the walls gave way to a series of steep
bluffs, fringed with barbed wire deep into the horizon. The view
reminded me of movies I had seen in school about detention centers built by the Japanese during their occupation.

Not far from the gate stood a guard station equipped with can-
nons. I was looking around in wide-eyed curiosity when the truck
stopped again. The gate closed behind us, and a group of guards
began walking toward the truck. Their uniforms were reminiscent of
those worn by the People's Army, only they were a slightly lighter
shade of khaki, and their four-pocket jackets extended straight to
their pants. Our guards provided them with the spelling our of
names, then we set off again. The next time we stopped was a quarter of an hour later. Outside, there was a great bustle; I could hear
voices, whispering. It was like a welcoming committee had gathered
in our honor. One of our guards then climbed down from the truck
and started shouting abuses. How brutally he spoke! How dare he
address people so crudely? The guard fired off so many orders and
insults, I grew panicked and began shaking. My father had to put his
hand on my shoulder to calm me down.

The guards then pulled the canvas cover off the truck and we all
stood up. I was still holding my aquarium in my arms. I had the
vague impression that this was to be a decisive moment. The canvas was like a theater curtain that had been prematurely drawn. A
new scene, indeed a new act, had begun, and none of us were ready
for it. I would have liked to know more about the roles we were
expected to play. But I didn't have long to inquire because the men
and women standing around the truck were already stepping for-

ward for a closer look. How frightfully filthy they all were, dressed like beggars, their hair caked and matted with dirt. Panic took hold of me again. Who were these people? Were they the same people I had just heard making all the commotion? Could it really be they whom the guards had addressed so brutally? To my astonishment, a number of them recognized my grandmother and came forward to greet her. As we stepped down from the truck, one old lady—a former friend, I suppose—ran up and gave her a hug, and for a long time the two women stood holding each other's hands, sighing deeply and crying.

"I was so worried when you disappeared," said my grandmother.

"No one told you?"

"We heard nothing."

"And now you're here, like me! After all we did for the Party!"

As I stood watching, two boys came up to me. I thought they were my age, but it turned out they were actually two years older.

"The camp is no place to grow big and strong," said one of them. "A lot of kids stop growing here."

The adults went on trading news and whispering in each others' ears, holding back the tears as best they could. What a sight these people made with their threadbare rags, their overgrown hair, their filth. How out of keeping their appearance seemed with the civility of their manner and their politeness toward the new arrivals. The welcome would probably have gone on for some time had not the guards intervened. They reestablished order in a wink, commanding all the prisoners back to their barracks and work details. That put an end to my somewhat abstract fascination, bringing me back to reality and my all-important fish. Alas, half of them were already dead. At a loss for what else to do, I started counting the victims. The few prisoners who had managed to tarry stepped closer and stared silently at the extraordinary spectacle standing among them: a child in the middle of the camp, crying softly over an aquarium in which floated, stomach up, the most fantastical assortment of exotic fish.

In a moment, a man who appeared to be the warden cut through the small crowd. "These things are going to stink to high heaven," he bellowed. "Go dump them somewhere far away!" He then turned to my parents and pointed toward a group of huts about a hundred yards off. "That's where you're living," he said, gesturing for us to follow. We had hardly walked ten paces when we were stopped by the sight of a man running toward us at full speed. It was my third uncle. He had already been in the camp for a week. The Security Force had picked him up at his conference. Before our arrival, he had been living in the bachelor's quarters, a very peculiar dwelling, of which more later. My grandmother—though she had hoped her youngest boy might escape the camps—felt a great joy at suddenly seeing him there, and as she kissed him, warm tears ran down her face.

We approached the designated hut. My father pushed the wooden door in silence. We joined him, and what we saw left us stunned. This was where we were going to live? Under a roof of bare wooden planks, with dried earth for walls, and packed dirt for our floor? The guards ordered a few prisoners to help us finish our resettlement. It didn't take long; all we had were our two dressers, a low table, our clothes, and 125 pounds of rice. It was painful to look at these furnishings, infused still with the memory of our luxurious Pyongyang apartment. In the heavy silence our eyes wandered among the accoutrements of the past and the bleak surroundings of the present.

The hut was a four-family building. Our unit, the largest of the four, had a partition down the middle splitting it into two rooms.

The dividing wall stopped short of the ceiling, so that a single bulb hanging directly above it could illuminate both spaces. I later discovered that the partition was built for the benefit of families who didn't get along; it was permissible to take it down. The camp also had smaller-sized huts that were constructed for two and three families which, due to their low roofs and little squat openings for doors, were usually referred to as "harmonicas." Every hut was surrounded with a patch of fenced-off dirt where the prisoners could grow whatever they wanted. Or rather whatever they could, for they worked so hard during the day, they had neither time nor energy at night for anything but sleep.

All of the camp's electricity was generated by a little hydroelectric plant located inside the camp's perimeter. The limitations of the system soon were apparent: the water froze in the wintertime and was too scant in the summer. Outages were therefore a frequent occurrence. Our immediate concern on our first night, however, was figuring out how to start a fire without matches or a lighter. Fortunately, our neighbors came by and taught us a few of the camp's basic survival skills. They demonstrated how to chop down a tree quickly and safely, how to keep a flame alive on a pine-resin-soaked wick, how to cook cornmeal over a wood fire, et cetera. There were no faucets in the huts, so all the water had to be drawn from the river that was a ten-minute walk—or a little longer on the way back, when the bucket was full. To a well-fed person these trips would be boring and uncomfortable but constitute an insurmountable test. Weak and undernourished as we would soon be, however, they were nothing short of exhausting. The other thing we didn't have was heating fuel. That was what we had used in Pyongyang, but no such luxuries existed in Yodok. Instead we had to forage for wood that was dry enough to catch fire. Our room had a wood-burning furnace that, when topped with a caldron, doubled for a stove. Preparing the food was the family's responsibility, and since Grandmother was old, the guards assigned her to this task. She had done well to bring a few kitchen things from Pyongyang: the only utensils the camp provided were beat-up mess tins.

Besides the huts, there were several large horseshoe-shaped buildings, which housed the single prisoners. My uncle told us they slept five or six to a room and seventy to one hundred per structure. Like the family units, these buildings were edged with small plots where prisoners could grow their own vegetables, but over the years, these areas kept shrinking. They first became the site for the buildings' common kitchens and two outhouses, and later for stables housing the bulls and cows used for drawing carts. In each single building, the guards selected one prisoner to be barracks chief and lord over his fellow singles. From the remaining prisoners, four were assigned to work in the kitchen. These were always three women and one man, the latter being largely responsible for gathering and hauling wood. Some of the singles were in Yodok because they belonged to criminal families. Others were just petty criminals: people who missed an official march, exhibited want of enthusiasm for the Great Leader, or lacked requisite zeal in their denunciation of traitors to the state. Such wrongdoers usually spared the prisons for hardened criminals. They were, however, kept under special surveillance and forbidden from leaving their hut at night.

The collection of ten huts that made up our immediate surroundings constituted what we prisoners called a "village," a word ill-fitted to the disorganized jumble of huts devoid of streets, a center, periphery, or official buildings. Formally, these settlements were known as "workers' groups," and each one was assigned a number for identification. Among ourselves, we shunned these cold, bureaucratic appellations and came up with a more poetic nomenclature of our own. Workers' group number 2 was the "Royal Pine Village," workers' group number 4, the "Chestnut Tree Village," and workers' group number 10—where we lived—was "The Village on the Plain."

Each village consolidated a specific category of detainees. Ours, which was built in 1974, was inhabited solely by former Japanese residents and their families. The segregation served as tacit recognition of our difficult integration into North Korean society, as well as a way of isolating all mention of the capitalist hell existing outside the country's borders. For the same reason we were also forbidden—under threat of severe punishment—from having any contact with prisoners from other villages. Furtive messages were occasionally exchanged, however, during campwide ceremonies or up in the mountains, where we were sent to gather medicinal herbs under slack surveillance by the guards. Our communications were usually confined to notes about the layout of the camp, as we worked to expand the limited picture handed down to us by camp veterans. We traded information about the population of the various villages, the severity of the guards, the availability of food, and so forth.

All this came later, though. On first arriving at Yodok, we were like sailors just landed on a desert island, still marked by our recently departed world, but obliged to rediscover the gestures of a more remote past: to grab an ax, chop down a tree, build a fire, and cook something into a meal. We didn't have much time: night would be falling soon, and in the dark we would be at a complete loss. My uncle, who knew the place a little better than the rest of us, offered to help. He went out and chopped down a small tree for firewood, but the green logs burned so piteously and raised so much smoke that one of our neighbors offered some of his own stock—along with the suggestion that we start working on a woodpile of our own.

The greatest challenge of the night was still before us, however. We needed to figure out how to cook rice over an open flame. The problem had never before presented itself, and Grandmother was not particularly focused on the task. I can still taste that first night's rice: half burned and half uncooked. And yet it was the cause of much envy in the camp; one bachelor sneaked up to our hut and offered to exchange a bag of corn for a bowl of the barely edible mess. It looked great, and I pleaded with Grandmother to accept it, but she refused. Though served with the improbable hope of raising our spirits, dinner was not a particularly joyous event. Grandmother soon announced that our 125 pounds of rice wouldn't last long at this rate and that our consumption would therefore have to be cut back. We had no choice but to agree. That night the family made a pledge to stay united, no matter what, and help each other out as much as we could. The next day we would be receiving our work detail; it would no doubt be difficult, but we would make it if we stuck together. They wouldn't keep us in such a place forever!

Did any of us truly believe that the future would be so simple, that our honorable resolutions would actually be enough to protect us from reality? We nevertheless acted as though we believed, though the facade of optimism and heroic resolutions began to wear that very night, as we tossed and turned sleeplessly on our mats. We had resolved to create a common front, but against what?

Early the next morning, the first thing I saw through our little window was the surrounding mountain range. Its slopes were draped to their middle in a thick cover of trees. The view was magnificent. I was incredibly carefree, thinking back on it, which I can only attribute to my very young age. I was delighted by the stunning natural views—rare sights for a city boy like me—and it was in a state of great excitement that I stepped outside and started off toward the river. Birds sang all around me, and the air was brisk and infused with the fragrance of freshly cut hay. Arriving at the river, I discovered that its waters ran very deep and had a beautiful bluish green tint. I stood gazing into it for a moment, trying to make out fish in the current, then headed back to the hut.

By the time I returned, everyone was already awake. I sensed that the mood was not right for bucolic evocations and that I would do well to keep my impressions of the natural environs to myself. A few minutes later my uncle left to look for dead wood and I joined him. Our harvest was a meager one: for the commodity was apparently much sought after.

On our way back, we crossed paths with a little boy. I was sure he was the same age as I, but he swore he was two years my senior. Despite what I was told the previous day—about camp life stunting a child's development—I couldn't help being incredulous. His name was Oh Jung-il, and he was a four-year veteran of our village of former Japanese residents. Making conversation, my uncle ventured a remark on the beauty of the landscape, noting that "at least we have that for consolation."

"You call this consolation?" the boy shot back at him. "Take a better look around. We're in the trough of a valley. It might be uneven and bumpy, but it's still a valley, and we're surrounded by high mountains. The day you arrived in the camp you must have seen the line of barbed wire running out from either side of the entrance. The truth is, they only need it in a few places, where the natural obstacles aren't drastic enough. In any case, it's impossible to lay barbed wire when the slopes are too steep. Not that it really matters, given that they've strung a metal wire all around the periphery, which sets off an alarm as soon as you touch it. If that's not enough, there are armed units on every mountaintop surveying the surrounding slopes."

From where we were standing, we couldn't see the electric wire, which apparently ran very close to the ground. As we squinted into the distance, Oh Jung-il went on.

"Besides the barbed wire and the military patrol, they also set traps like for wild animals. They dig ditches, plant them with rows of sharpened stakes, then camouflage them with branches. Just a few things you should know," he continued, giggling, "in case you ever get an itch to make a run for it."

The one advantage an escaping prisoner did have was a twelve-hour jump on his pursuers. Roll calls were held every six hours, but the guards only began investigating after they noticed two consecutive absences.

"Role call? When? Where?"

"You're totally clueless," responded the kid, laughing. "There are three role calls at Yodok camp, at five-thirty A.M., at noon, and at six-thirty P.M. They take place in front of the supply office, where work details are assigned to the different groups. Role calls last half an hour regardless of the weather. Only people with sick certificates are excused. Otherwise, everyone has to go, and you get punished if you don't, or if you show up late."

The kid then returned to the subject of escape, which was clearly dear to his heart. Only once had he heard the sirens go off and seen the security agents form into search parties and head up into the mountains. It took a while, but they eventually came down with their prey. The escaping prisoner had been stopped midcourse, well short of the summits he had hoped might spell freedom. He was tortured for a week or two, then executed.

"The punishment for attempted escape is execution. No exceptions. The guards make the whole village come out to watch it. . . . So given all that, I have a hard time seeing these mountains as very beautiful."

We were silent, but the look on our faces must have communicated our horror. The boy noticed. Feeling a little guilty, perhaps, he tried to say something friendly and offer us a few bits of advice, which showed he was actually a nice kid whose humanity was still very much alive.

"Yeah," he went on, "you gotta be really crazy to try to escape. On the other hand, sometimes you gotta be even crazier to stay, especially if you're all alone, without family or friends. The work is hard, and there's hardly ever enough food to take the edge off your hunger. . . . You'll have to stick together, help each other out—and, remember, don't trust anyone."

"And you," the boy said, turning to me, "you'll be amazed at what they call school here. Anyway, good luck to you."

His back was already turned and he was walking away, a towering bundle of grass balanced precipitously atop his head. We had spent too long talking and needed to hurry back. The guards had told us that at eight that morning our brigade leader would come by to explain the camp's work details and rules of conduct. It was stressed that the whole family should be present. In North Korea—as I later learned was the case in the Soviet Union and Nazi Germany— camp guards aren't satisfied to do all the surveillance themselves: they designate prisoners, unwilling ones sometimes, to become local chiefs and carry out responsibilities the police can't execute on their own. They collect information and have the power to punish recalcitrants, most notably by denouncing them to their superiors. The brigade chiefs are important links in the chain of command between the camp's authorities and the common detainee. They each supervise about ten work teams and only need to work half time themselves.

The brigade leader was already there by the time my uncle and I got back to the hut. Standing alongside a guard, his companion on these missions, he was giving my family a rundown of the camp's work rules. Grandmother would be the only one exempt from working, it being her responsibility to stay home and cook for the rest of us. The routine for my sister and me was school in the morning and manual labor in the afternoon. There would also be the common chores of chopping wood and hauling logs, growing corn, pulling weeds, and so forth, as well as obligatory participation in the Party's recently initiated campaign for the foraging of wild ginseng in the mountains, a project sure to be "close to our hearts," given our desire to redeem our bad conduct. The camp's various work details were assigned to five-prisoner work teams, each with its own production quota. Work details were handed down from the brigade leader to the team leader and from him to the other members of the team. The brigade leader himself was subordinate to a prisoner-overseer, who was chosen by the authorities to represent the village as a whole. While exempt from performing any physical labor, the overseer was responsible for surveying the prisoners and drawing up reports. If his workload ever became too burdensome, a second overseer could be assigned to assist him. The brigade leader who was explaining all this to us never mentioned the criteria used for selecting the overseer, but I was later able to divine this information for myself: the man's requirements were to be burly—so to be physically menacing—and to have a general propensity for wholehearted collaboration with the camp's authorities. With these qualities as the cornerstone of his character, it is no surprise that the overseer tended to be more severe than even the guards—and more universally loathed by his fellow prisoners. The network of collaboration didn't end with him. There was also a "delegate" to help the agents prepare and organize work details; two statisticians to track the progress of various harvests (of wood, grains, etc.); and two general administrators: one to oversee the distribution of food, tools, and uniforms, and the other to organize special ceremonies.

When the brigade leader had finished his orientation, the guard stepped forward to say his piece.

"You people don't deserve to live," he announced, "but the Party and our Great Leader have given you a chance to redeem yourselves. Don't squander it and don't disappoint him. We will discuss all this further at our next meeting for criticism and self-criticism."

The two then left without another word, which was a little encouraging. The guard really scared me. I later learned to distinguish the real zealots—the ones who lay in wait for a word or a look that might betray the family criminality—from those you could talk to. The guards were almost all uneducated, rough people, of a generally bad character. There were a few exceptions, of course, but they could never stand their assignment for long. Eventually the camp's atmosphere would get to them, and they would ask to be transferred elsewhere.

To become a guard at a place like Yodok, the first requirement was having a good background—in other words, being from a family of peasants or of poor workers. Next, you had to have no "anti-Communist criminals" in your family as far as your first cousins. You were then judged on your personal qualities, namely, your physical strength and your degree of political orthodoxy. If everything still checked out, you would be admitted into the training program required for serving at a camp.

The guards moved into Yodok with their families and lived in a small barrack near the camp's main entrance. Their children attended a school on the camp grounds—a separate one from ours, of course, it being crucial to separate the wheat from the chaff. Theirs was a real school, open more than just the mornings, with real teachers instead of vicious brutes. The guards' kids were treated as well as Pyongyang residents and received an education that was every bit as good. As the offspring of criminals, we weren't even allowed to meet these children. On a couple of occasions, though, I did manage to catch a glimpse of them. I remember how surprised I was the first time. It was September 1979 and I was working in a field abutting their school. I heard a cry of joy and looked up to see them in the yard. I was fascinated by their energy, the cleanliness of their clothes, their ruddy faces and well-cropped hair, all of which made them seem so different from the creature I had become.

During his morning visit, the brigade leader had assigned my father and uncle to an agricultural work team, to which they were to report at 6:00 A.M. the next day, the same time my sister and I were to be in school. Our half workday would begin at 1:00 P.M. The schedule would remain unchanged until we reached the age of fifteen, at which point we would be considered adults and assigned to full work duty. Before our new routine could begin, however, we had to go to the supply office for our uniforms. We all showed up there together to try on the meager selections of hand-me-downs.

The experience left us all feeling a little ashamed. As we shed our old clothes, we could feel our former civilian lives slipping away, those lives in which we wore ties and clean shirts, briefs and comfortable socks. From this point forward, our wardrobes would consist of a purple jacket and a pair of pants, both coarsely sewn from a rough, heavy cloth. The uniforms were fitted with a great number of buttons and resembled the Chinese prison outfits I later saw on television and in the movies. Wearing this uniform for the first time was strange enough, but seeing my father and sister in them was stranger still. When it rained a few weeks later, we were in for another unpleasant discovery: the clothes shrank as soon as they got wet. Now they weren't just uncomfortable, they were downright ridiculous, too. Not that any of the veteran detainees ever noticed. These uniforms were distributed to us in mid-August and were meant to serve us through the entire year. A few prisoners told me the camp had precise rules regulating distribution of linen and uniforms. If these rules existed, they certainly weren't followed while I was there. In all my time in Yodok, I only received uniforms twice, and though they quickly came apart, they were all I had to wear—day after day, year after year, in field, mine, forest, and mountain.

During our years of detention, rags were often the only clothing we had. Our garments eventually reached such a repulsive state that the guards had no choice but to let us wear our old clothes from the "outside." It wasn't long before these became so tattered and grimy as to be indistinguishable from our uniforms. After a few months in the camp, the appearance of our rags bothered us no more than they did anybody else. The only thing that mattered was keeping warm. When the winter cold set in, we put on everything we could get our hands on, hoping against hope that the layers of rags might protect us. We were also constantly on the lookout for ways to steal more clothes. Working on a funeral crew, we never buried a corpse without first stripping it naked. Apart from the cold, the worst part was underwear. The camp authorities provided us with briefs and undershirts, but their cloth was so rough that it rasped our skin, causing us to itch and sometimes to develop open wounds, such that we soon found it preferable to go without them. I ultimately came up with the idea of recycling my old tattered briefs into linings, sewing them to the inside of my camp-issued underwear. As for socks, our annual quota of one pair never lasted long, despite my grandmother's ceaseless and often miraculous darning.

At night, after a brief dinner of corn, we all scrambled immediately off to bed, thinking of the day to come, our first day of work in the camp, a day that would surely be difficult. For me it was simply horrible.

여섯

SIX

THE WILD BOAR: A
TEACHER ARMED AND
READY TO STRIKE

Grandmother woke me up just as the sun was beginning to rise.
Here at Yodok, there could be no question of arguing or of feigning
sleep. I rolled out of bed under the pallid light of our solitary bulb. I
put on my horrible uniform, swallowed another little helping of corn,
and walked off to my assigned assembly location. By the time I
arrived, several of the children were already there waiting. They all
stared at me with wide, curious eyes. Several minutes passed, then a
few students—I supposed them to be delegates of some sort—got us
into rows and marched us toward the school, leading us in a rendition of "The Song of Kim Il-sung," which I knew from my days at the
People's School in Pyongyang. Unfortunately, our singing on this
morning was judged too reserved by the teachers waiting for us at the
school entrance and we were ordered to back up ten yards and take
the march and song again with more vigor.

The school was a square compound composed of two facing buildings joined on either side by a wall. A flower bed and a lawn stretched between the buildings. The classrooms were floor-heated in the traditional Korean manner, but only when the temperature dropped below 14°F. Above the blackboards, dominating every classroom, hung the portraits of Kim Il-sung and Kim Jong-il. The school's rickety collection of desks were jerry-built things, nailed together by prisoners from leftover building materials. Since North Korea has always maintained that war is imminent and that enemies are everywhere, the country is in a constant state of alert. Little surprise, then, that our school buildings were under twenty-four-hour surveillance. To make this oversight possible, two annexes were added to the back of the buildings. The first housed the on-duty schoolmaster, while the second, slightly larger building lodged the twelve student guards who worked on twelve-hour shifts. A little farther off was the little building that held the Kim Il-sung Room, a sort of shrine filled with posters, books, and photos honoring the exploits of the Great Leader. Behind the annexes was a row of warrens that caged the school's rabbits.

In September 1977, I was beginning my final year of grammar school. (In North Korea, primary education lasts four years and is followed by five years of middle school.) At Yodok, all the kids from several neighboring villages were placed to one of two mixed-level classes with fifty students each. We began our school day by sweeping and mopping the classroom floor. After this little exercise was done, at around seven, the schoolmaster gave us our morning assignment. For the first hour, students were supposed to get in groups and review the previous day's lesson. Since I was new, I had nothing to do but sit and wait. The review session was followed by lessons in Korean, mathematics, biology, and, finally, the politics of the Party, which was the teacher's clear favorite. The latter class essentially consisted of repeating formulas I'd been mouthing my entire life, about the advantages of the brilliant "Juche" ideology extolling the self-sufficiency of the Korean community, whose singular existence was animated by the spirit of our one and only Great Leader. In this course as in the others, I learned little I did not already know. Each lesson lasted fifty minutes and was followed by a ten-minute break. Classes were over by noon.

I had teachers at Yodok who actually took their jobs seriously. Most teachers, however, showed a total disregard for our well-being, sometimes even letting us nap with our heads on our desks under the pretense that this was teaching us self-sufficiency and discipline. Apart from the ideological regime, which was more or less the same everywhere in North Korea, there was simply no comparison between the lives of Yodok students and those of students on the outside.

Our teachers generally addressed us in the harshest, crudest manner. Instead of using our first or last names, they blurted things like "Hey, you, in the back of the room! Hey, you, the idiot in the third row! Hey, you, son of a whore." It was also common for them to beat us. That came as quite a discovery for me. Unlike the teachers I'd had in Pyongyang—who were attentive, patient, and devoted—my instructors at Yodok were simply brutes, whose primary concern was crushing "counterrevolutionary vermin"—or rather the offspring of counterrevolutionary vermin, which to them amounted to the same thing.

The camp had many difficult times in store—the death of good friends, my grandmother's illnesses, my frostbite, the obligatory witnessing of public executions—but by the time these things happened, I'd had experiences to help me absorb the shock. No good is ever expected of an accident or an illness or an execution. But a child of ten can well expect some good to come from school, such as friends and teachers who care for him and help him discover things, who listen and encourage. Any such hope I might have had was betrayed the first day I walked through the classroom door. Our teacher, revolver at his side, hollered at us at the slightest irritation and quickly graduated to insulting and beating.

Newly arrived and still unfamiliar with what passed for good behavior, I was overanxious to win the teacher's good graces and demonstrate my superiority over the rest of the class. Perhaps the other kids in the room really were bad eggs, but I certainly wasn't. My grandmother had been a member of the National Assembly, and my grandfather had given his entire fortune to the Party. To show I was one of Kim Il-sung's good soldiers, I kept asking questions and putting in my two cents whenever possible.

What a mistake! As the teacher was lecturing about the Namhodu conference and Kim Il-sung's brilliant speech of April 27, 1936, I became aware that he was confusing the circumstances surrounding this address with the intrigues of the Dahongdan conference. I raised my hand and asked him about the possible confusion. The man with the revolver walked over with a heavy step and slapped me hard across the face. There was a burst of laughter in the room. The new guy had just got his first lesson. I was terror stricken—though more outraged than sad, more hate-filled than despairing. I decided that I would do everything in my power to undermine that vile brute who was passing himself off as a teacher. I would do like the others and sit there without saying a word. Yet my silent compact would prove a weak palliative against the lasting pain of that episode. In receiving that slap I grasped that my life had fallen into a "nasty place," to recall the phrase of my former Pyongyang comrades.

The break with my former world didn't coincide with my arrival
at the camp. In some respects, the place itself was not to blame. I
could sometimes forget my detention and let myself be transported
by the pleasure of being in the country. The river and the distant
mountains were often a source of relief and consolation. But that
first day of class remains a horrible memory. I felt something tear
inside me then—something that connected me to the only other
life I had known. From then on, I felt the same fear in front of certain teachers as I had felt the day of our arrival, when from inside
the truck I heard the guards shouting abuses at the people clamor-
ing to see us, the new criminals. I had been made to believe—and
had indeed wanted to believe—that the Democratic People's
Republic of Korea was the best country in the world. I looked up to
Kim Il-sung as a god. Yet here were armed teachers beating and
insulting their student charges.

Over the course of my detention, I had half a dozen male teachers
and two female teachers, both of whom were the wives of guards. Of
all, only one deserved the title of instructor. The worst was the one
we called the Wild Boar—the very same who had taken such exception to my knowledge of the Namhodu conference. Almost as ruth-
less was Pak Tae-seu, a.k.a. the Old Fox, who sometimes punished
his students by making them stand naked in the courtyard all day
with their hands behind their backs. We hated him so much we once
got up the courage to damage his bicycle. To get us to denounce the
culprits, he confined us all to our huts. When that didn't work, he
tried threats and thrashings and extra hours of work at night, when
our sole desire in life was to sleep. But we never cracked.

One of the most common forms of school punishment was
latrine duty. There were always two monitors—fellow prisoners
both—who stood at the school entrance to watch over the arriving
students and pick out the latecomers. A student who was tardy

could expect to get a week's worth of latrine duty, which consisted of cleaning the stalls or emptying the septic tanks. The tanks had to be emptied once a year, and if there was a dearth of students requiring punishment, the teachers would choose kids at random.

One time a friend of mine from class started complaining to us because he'd been picked for the nasty job several times in a row. "I'm always the one," he whined. "Don't the teachers have anything better for us to do? It's probably because they like shit!" Someone must have gone to squeal to the Wild Boar, because a minute later we saw him walking toward us looking mad as hell. He grabbed the guilty student and started beating him savagely, first punching him with his clenched fists, then kicking him. Battered and wobbly-legged, the boy fell into the septic tank, where he remained trapped for a long time, unable to find a foothold or get anyone to reach in and help him. Content with his work, the teacher lost interest and walked away. After a long struggle, my friend managed to reach the edge and climb out, but he was in such a sad state that no one wanted to help him wash up or bandage his wounds. A few days later he died. We never quite knew of what. But the story has an epilogue: a few days later, his mother went to see the teacher, weeping and asking for her son back. The Wild Boar calmly replied that the boy had said revolting things and deserved what punishment he got. As for his death, well, that wasn't his responsibility. And then he kicked the mother out!

The Wild Boar treated us more like animals than children—which, he never failed to remind us, was already a considerable indulgence on his part: "Since your parents are counterrevolutionaries, they deserve to die, and you, their children, along with them. Fortunately for you, the Party is kind and its Great Leader magnanimous. He has granted you a reprieve and the chance to redeem yourselves. You should be grateful, but instead you commit further offenses! Commit too many and you will not be forgiven!" We would all lower our eyes, wishing for our torturer's death. Boys and girls were equal beneficiaries of his undiscriminating brutality and his favorite punishment, which consisted of ordering a student down on all fours and making him or her crawl in front of the class, saying, "I'm a dog . . . I'm a dog. . . ."

Our two women teachers were considerably less rough. We christened one of them, a rotund lady in her fifties, the Chinese Cabbage. Though she was stronger than almost any of the male teachers, she was less severe in her beatings. She did have her forte, however: a nasty pinch that left a big blue patch on your skin. The desire to practice her little specialty could overtake her at any moment, which taught us always to keep out of her reach. The other woman teacher was younger, around thirty years old. She wasn't mean, but she tried to make it seem as if she was. She often yelled at the students, but there was rarely any anger in her voice. To punctuate her shouting frenzies, she would sometimes hit us on the hands with her ruler, but her blows had no more weight than her yelling. Alas, she left the camp after two years to bring a child into the world. Apart from these women and another teacher I'm still grateful to, the teachers were all brutes. The Wild Boar, with his beatings and his outbursts of unbounded rage, was truly disturbed. The Old Fox, for his part, practiced a cruelty that was nothing short of sadistic. He battered us with method, an adept technician of suffering, always searching for a way to maximize pain. When our hands were stained black from peeling walnuts, for example, he would make us clean them by rubbing them back and forth across the ground. And if ever we didn't rub hard enough, he crushed our hands beneath his boot.

Trust between student and teacher was utterly impossible under such conditions. As for the teacher who caused our friend's death, the only feeling that connected us to him was unalloyed hatred. We couldn't stand the arrogance of these would-be pedagogues, their ridiculous vanity as they tooled around the camp perched on their bicycles. I remember the winter day when we saw the teacher we called the Youngster arrive in the courtyard on his brand-new bike. He tried to show off by coming to a skidding stop, but instead slipped and went flying into the mud. We laughed to high heaven. Crimson with rage, the idiot started chasing us around with a stick—as local custom demanded. All the guards had a right to one of these bikes, which were called Seagulls. Owning a Seagull was a mark of distinction, a symbol of the guards' superiority over the lowly prisoners, who had to shuffle around the camp in bad shoes or with rags tied around their feet. Unlike most North Korean–made products, the Seagulls, which were produced in the Susong prison, were of very good quality—good enough, in fact, to compete on the international market. They usually sold for 3,000 won (i.e., $40 on the black market, or ten times that counting by the official exchange rate). The Chinese bikes, by comparison, cost 2,000 won, while the Japanese models generally ran in the 10,000-won range. If the Susong prison plant ever exceeded its quota, the surplus bikes were sold for only 1,500 won. First in line for these were the relatives of security agents and camp and prison guards. They all doted on their bikes, which is exactly why we decided to vandalize Old Fox's beloved machine.

These childish capers, so like those pulled off by children every-where around the world, could mean serious trouble in Yodok. Such was the case when the Wild Boar asked one of us—his name was Kim Chae-yu—to watch his Seagull while he went to a teacher's meeting. As soon as Wild Boar had turned his back, we all started begging Kim to let us take a few laps on the bike. It took some work, but he finally ceded. I was the fifth to take a spin and was more than a little proud to be peddling around on that magnificent machine, though by the time my turn came the bike was not looking that great. The first kid had only been riding a minute or so when he took a fall and bent one of the mud guards. We managed to pull it back with our hands, but the dent was noticeable. The second rider managed to complete his laps without incident, but then the third kid broke a spoke, and all of us were being very careless about riding through mud and puddles. We were in full frivolity when Wild Boar came back earlier than expected. He immediately started beating Kim Chae-yu, and when he was done with him, he kicked the rest of us. The real punishment, however, was a week of supplementary night work, during which we were made to dig ditches, then fill them with rocks, then dig new ditches and fill them with the dirt from the first ditch, and so on. Like in a bad dream.

Classes ended at noon. We had an hour to rest and eat the cornmeal we brought from home in a mess kit. Afterward we worked outdoors under the teacher's supervision. That's how I learned to plant rice, grow corn, and chop down trees. My first work assignment was on a team that assisted adults who were logging up in the mountains. We were charged with hauling the logs down to the village, where another group of adults cut the wood into small pieces, about a meter long, and loaded them into a truck. The logs were terribly heavy, even with two of us carrying them, and the place where the trees were being felled was three or four kilometers from the village. To fill our daily quota, we had to finish twelve round trips each, which added up to about forty kilometers, with a log on our shoulder half the way. The work would have been exhausting for the heartiest of children; and for a city boy like me, for whom this was a first introduction to physical labor, it was simply impossible. I was dead on my feet by the third trip and had to ask the kid working with me to stop a minute so I could catch my breath. He grumblingly agreed. I sat down. In an instant, a black curtain descended before my eyes and I fell to the ground. I was out for about an hour. When I came to I was surrounded by the kids in my work group, who were all furious with me.

Like the adults, we worked in groups of five. If illness or physical incapacity caused one of the detainees to lag, the whole group fell behind and risked being penalized. There was no such thing as individual responsibility: one's work only counted as part of the collective output. As long as a team's quota hadn't been reached, none of its members could return to the village, no matter how old or tired or sick they might be. Workers needed to remain with their group, and the group needed to meet its quota. The policy had the effect of breeding animosity among the detainees and destroying any solidarity that might serve as moral balm. This might have been the very reason for the policy's existence. The guards could basically sit back and relax: the prisoners were forced to create a system of self-surveillance, which while perfectly effective at maintaining order, required little outside intervention.

It's easy to imagine how angry my comrades were with me that afternoon. Some of them accused me of putting on an act and even started kicking me, disguising their blows as friendly pick-me-ups to rouse me from my stupor. The next day the teacher assigned me to an easier detail: keeping track of the round trips completed by the others. But it wasn't long before I was again judged ready for hard labor.

일곱

SEVEN

DEATH OF A BLACK CHAMPION

My first months at Yodok were among the most difficult. I had to adjust to a life without comforts, to restrictions on my time, to extreme physical exertion, and to unfamiliar food. And I had to do it in relative solitude, for in a place like Yodok, rare are the bonds of friendship and solidarity.

Our arrival had initially constituted a major event in the lives of Yodok's detainees, a chance to reestablish contact with the outside world. Talking to a newly arrived prisoner was like feeling a fresh wind from the world beyond their valley prison. But in the beginning I cringed at getting too close to the other detainees. Their faces were ugly, they had missing teeth, their hair was caked together and overgrown, and they were all filthy as animals. Yet more striking than their physical appearance was the aura of weakness that oozed from their every pore. Their weariness and dejection seemed the root of their neglect—these and a pervasive sense of desperation, which they were perhaps more adept at dissimulating. None of them made any effort to look presentable. It was clear that they bathed rarely, if at all, and that the work of laundering was usually left to the rain and snow.

During the first days of my detention, I met a kid who wore black socks. At least that's what I thought until I realized his socks in fact were an incredible layer of dirt and grime. I, too, would one day wear such "socks." I'm still grateful to my grandmother for forcing us to wash our hands and feet whenever we had a little time and energy. It was a way of resisting the imposed conditions and the feelings of exhaustion and self-loathing they engendered.

My father, uncle, and sister seemed as exhausted as I. When we returned to our hut at night and sat around the little low table eating our corn, hardly anyone said a word. As soon as we were done eating, we hurried off to bed, knowing instinctively that to survive here, we'd need to recuperate all the strength we could.

Still, before getting into bed, I would spend a few minutes hunched over my aquarium. It seemed too large now for the three or four fish that still clung to life. It mattered little that I changed their water and that I provided them food by catching insects during my work. They were having as hard a time at Yodok as I was. Eventually there was only one survivor: a black fish who had succeeded in adjusting to his catch-as-catch-can diet. As temperatures dropped throughout November, he continued to hold strong; then he held out through December, too. To keep the aquarium from freezing over, I wrapped it in rags and asked Grandmother to move it near the stove whenever she did any cooking. Yet winter deepened, my efforts seemed every day more hopeless. The temperature soon fell below freezing in our hut, and we spent our nights shivering in our blankets.

Despite all my cares, the black champion died. Over the last weeks of summer I had gathered roaches, dragonflies, silkworms, and any other bugs that might pass for fish food. I had dried these in the sun and ground them into a powder. My fish accepted the food, but the cold got the better of him. Seeing his lifeless body floating on the surface of the water filled me with great sadness. Yet distraught I wasn't. By this time I was struggling with the problem of my own survival and had little energy left for grieving. What I was staring at was the final dissolution of my former life: a door that was closing. That fish had known our life in Pyongyang and, from time to time, he reminded me of the pebbles, sand, and diptychs I had bought at the store around the corner from our house. With his death, my former world had taken another step.

The retreat of that other universe was also manifested in my mother's absence, which was growing ever longer. In the beginning, I hardly thought of her. Our days were so full, we hadn't time to think about anyone, and at night we were so tired I barely had the energy left to utter her name. The memories didn't come on their own, and I had no desire to help them along. Yet as the days and weeks passed, my sister and I longed more and more for Mother's return. When we asked Grandmother about it, she pleaded ignorance. Father, for his part, counseled patience, but he acted like someone who no longer believed his own words.

I feel almost guilty complaining publicly about the life I led at Yodok. Yes, guilty, for Yodok is by no means the toughest camp in North Korea. Far worse exist, and they are shrouded in such secrecy that for a long time it was impossible to talk about them with any precision. Rumors about these places circulated constantly at Yodok, but firsthand accounts were rare. Most of the prisoners in these camps were irredeemables serving life sentences. There were a few exceptions, however, and they sometimes got transferred to Yodok. According to them, our camp was paradise compared to the others. Such judgments were always difficult for us to believe, and we would press these rare birds for more details. They said that the guards in other camps would breathe down their necks, pushing them to work ever harder, and that they had Kalachnikovs slung over their shoulders, ready to fire at the slightest hint of provocation. At Yodok, the guards only had revolvers, and these rarely came out of their holsters. The surveillance, furthermore, was not always that close. The guards at Yodok never let their work put them out. The only thing they cared about was our production quota. Harassing inmates for its own sake was rarely part of the program.

Like the irredeemables in Yodok, the inmates of the other hard-labor camps were members of landholding families, capitalists, U.S. or South Korean agents, Christians, or members of purged Party circles deemed noxious to the state. The various prisoners were given the same treatment, regardless of their crime. Unlike Yodok's redeemable population, who stopped work early on bad-weather days, the irredeemables labored equally long hours during the winter and summer months. The men and the women lived separately and were grouped according to their health and vigor, with the strongest prisoners assigned to the most backbreaking work. Their children received an education that was even less worthy of that title than what we had. After barely three years of middle school, the kids were classified as adults and assigned to fatigue duty from morning until night. At Yodok, the children of irredeemables had their own schools, and we were strictly forbidden from mixing. Their clothes, too, were more threadbare, torn, and dirty than anything we wore. A final detail: they were all given special haircuts, which marked them as lifers, and made it impossible for them to pass for citizens if they ever tried to escape.

Yodok and the hard-labor camps did have several points in common, the first of these being the snitches. During the first days and weeks of our detention, my father and uncle felt most oppressed by the physical demands of forced labor and the looming threat of punishment. The slightest wrong move, it seemed, could mean extra work or a stint of solitary confinement in a sweatbox. This fear, they soon realized, was the consequence of the network of snitches that pervaded the camp. The informants were at every turn. There was no one to confide in, no way to tell who was who. The veteran prisoners sometimes laughed at my father and uncle because of all the naïve questions they asked, which only made them more depressed. The only advice their fellow prisoners could offer was to have patience: they would learn to pick out the snitches soon enough. Until then, they would do well to keep their thoughts to themselves. The camp's common wisdom turned out to be true. Within a few months, we all developed a sixth sense—a snitch radar, if you will—that told us who could be trusted and who could not. Yet a snitch is not necessarily a bad guy. The prisoner is usually picked for the job without being asked his or her opinion, and, in most cases, the honor is not one for which he or she is proud.

Another similarity between Yodok and the hard-labor camps was the layout. Many people tended to imagine concentration camps as confined spaces surrounded by barbed wire and watch towers. In fact, Yodok is only one of many expansive reservations where fields, rivers, and hills take the place of man-made obstacles. Since its opening in 1959, it has been the system's largest camp. The idea for the prison was born when North Korea's defense minister visited the area and was impressed by its topography. A little later the government trucked in several squads of prisoners to build a few permanent structures—surveillance posts, living quarters for guards and their families, workshops, schools—then had them hammer together the remaining boards to make the villages. Once that was done, all that remained was to seal off the mouth of the valley. My "village" lay a day's walk—about twenty-five miles—from the foot of the surrounding mountains, which marked the edge of the camp. I was able to assess this distance during an authorized work outing to the mountain's lower slopes. Subsequent assignments allowed me to expand my picture of the general layout, but, since permission to move widely was rarely granted, I had limited knowledge of areas beyond my usual work zone.

I would be dishonest to claim exhaustive knowledge of Yodok, and I am still annoyed by my ignorance of the place where I lived for so long.

Our isolation seemed almost normal to us. We also knew that isolation was a feeling shared by prisoners everywhere, throughout the ages. Yet unlike in many prisons, we were not allowed to receive packages. (I didn't receive a single package during my entire stay.) The feeling of being isolated in the very place where I lived, to the point of not knowing who else was there or even where the camp was located, seemed particularly inhumane. It wasn't just a way of keeping me in the dark about where I was, it was a means of attacking my identity. After a decade in Yodok, my knowledge of the camp boils down to this: of Yodok's ten villages, four were for redeemables and six were for irredeemables, or political criminals. The latter group lived in a high-security zone that was separated from ours by several hills, as well as by rows of barbed wire rolled out along the valley's floor.

The irredeemables were all lifers. They knew they were never leaving the camp. No matter how long their hearts continued to pump, or their lungs to breathe, they would never again live as citizens. Their children, too, would suffer this fate. As the official propaganda never tired of reminding us, it was necessary to "desiccate the seedlings of counterrevolution, pull them out by their roots, exterminate every last one of them." That's the actual word the North Korean authorities used: exterminate—*myulhada*. These prisoners were tossed into a world of phantoms and nonentities, a world so devoid of hope it didn't even require its citizens to display portraits of Kim Il-sung and Kim Jong-il, or to learn the "lessons of Kim Il-sung's Revolution," or to attend sessions for criticism and self-criticism. Painful and absurd as the latter were, such requirements were grudging admissions that the people subjected to them were still citizens worthy of reeducation. They had run astray of the Party's path, but they might yet be brought back into the fold. The same could not be said for the irredeemables. To the Party and the socialist state, they were perfect zeros, worthy at best of supplying labor until their dying days. At Yodok, they represented approximately 70 percent of the camp's population.

The North Korean state separated even the irredeemables into different categories. I never learned what sort of criteria they used, but several detainees affirmed that certain irredeemables were condemned to work details so difficult and brutal that they soon died. These unfortunates were usually sent to large, isolated work sites, where they worked under a cloak of total secrecy building military complexes or assembling sensitive products such as missiles or other sophisticated munitions. In North Korea, such work is never entrusted to common citizens, or even to detainees who have a chance of one day getting out. Military secrets were best left to the irredeemables, who could take them to their graves. The system constitutes an important source of savings for the state: not only did it conserve the executioners' bullets, it furnishes from a labor force that demanded no salary and very little food.

There were various rumors in the camp about irredeemables who had engaged in savage, desperate revolts. Were they true stories or fantasies of revenge? According to one often-repeated story, a few years before our arrival at Yodok, the irredeemables held in the neighboring zone went on a rampage and killed a number of guards with axes, sickles, and pitchforks. The army was called in and immediately encircled the camp before any of the convicts could escape. It was said that no quarter was given to the male prisoners. This might explain why, by the time I arrived in Yodok, the high-security zone was filled mostly with old people, women, and children.

After meeting a few irredeemables, I lost any lingering doubt I might have had about the reality of this and other rumored rebellions. These prisoners' states of mind were so estranged from ordinary human thinking. In my part of the camp, the detainees still held to the hope of getting out one day. They set their teeth, suffered in silence, tried to hold out. Hope clung to their bodies even when it seemed to abandon their minds. But those in the high-security zone harbored no hope of returning to normal life. What reason could they have for patience? They must have thought—like Karl Marx's own proletariat—that they had only their chains to lose. In a life so grim, death was the only future close at hand.

여덟

CORN, ROACHES, AND
SNAKE BRANDY

My first winter in the camp was very trying, especially January and February of 1978. It wasn't school that was the problem anymore—that slap I got for knowing too much about the life of Kim Il-sung had taught me how to keep my mouth shut. I had also grown accustomed to the afterschool work of felling and hauling trees, so that wasn't the problem either. No, the greatest difficulty now had to do with nourishment. I was always hungry and had problems digesting the little food I did get. Our meals were so unchanging they started to make me sick. Grandmother noticed what was happening and, to break the monotony, sometimes cooked me some of our remaining rice. But she had resolved to make our little stock—the one buffer we had against extreme deprivation—last as long as possible, and would never cede to my pleas for more.

Corn was always on the menu: sometimes it was accented with the herbs Grandmother made us gather; sometimes it was plain;

sometimes it was mixed with acorn paste, which was every bit as bland as the corn. The acorns first had to be boiled and crushed into a paste, then molded into a block, and finally set out to dry and harden. After that, small bits of the block could be broken off and mixed with water and salt. From beginning to end, the process took several days.

We also created our own variation of *oksusupap*, a traditional dish of rice and corn. We used the camp's flour mill to crush the dried corn kernels into rice-sized bits, which we then boiled in water. A soup of dried vegetables sometimes interrupted our daily diet of corn, and once in a great while we would have a fish. We could only catch these when the guards weren't around, because fishing was banned at Yodok. The guards—straight-faced as ever—said that the rule existed to protect the environment. A few of the craftier inmates were nevertheless able to assemble complete fishing rigs with corks, shot, and hooks. On the camp's meager black market, a good line sold for about two pounds of corn, which wasn't all that much considering how much we valued a fish. Our camp rations were never plentiful enough to leave us feeling satiated. And the way we attacked our meals! Never exchanging a word. Just grunting, like people who had forgotten all their good manners.

We had brought kitchen utensils with us from Pyongyang, but they soon broke or wore out, at which point we had to use the mess tins distributed by the camp. Easily dented and immediately blackened by the open flames, they were ugly as could be. Yet what choice did we have? We had to make them last as long as possible, filling the holes with whatever we had at our disposal, or soldering them at the camp's welding shop. The most useful utensil we had was a kind of gourd that was easily carried on one's person. It was perfect for holding a frog or a salamander caught during the day. If we managed to steal some corn during our fieldwork, the gourd could also double as a cooking utensil. To prevent the guards from noticing our fire, we would use wood charcoal, which burns without smoking. Our favorite dish was a sort of grated corn chowder. If one of the kids from our work team succeeded in slipping into the cornfields unnoticed, the rest of us would ratchet up our production to help cover for the absentee while he stole a few ears of corn and prepared the soup. When I was ten years old, I was the smallest kid in my group and the one to whom this mission generally fell. I was good at it and had quite a successful streak. But one day I was caught. Fortunately, the guard decided a sound beating was punishment enough, and he refrained from assigning me extra work. I was on probation, however, and the next time my group picked me for a mission, I was so scared I was shaking. I'm still a little nostalgic for that dish—in spite of everything. I've had it several times since Yodok, but I've never been able to rediscover the taste it had in the camp. My last attempt was when I bought it in a fancy department store, but the results were disappointing and I haven't tried since.

Two events always gave the camp a morale boost: heavy rains and the launching of new education campaigns. Both meant a break from our usual existence as beasts of burden. The campaigns for the study of Kim Il-sung's thought took place in a large room on the village grounds. The program usually consisted of a Party official reading out loud from an article in *Rodong Sinmun*, the Party newspaper, which was supposed to incite us to new heights of political devotion. The reading was punctuated by short paraphrases—which the Party official thought of as commentary.

When heavy rains made it impossible for us to work outside, we were sent to one of the shops to repair tools or weave baskets. We felt less tired on these days and more like ourselves. Dinnertime was vaguely reminiscent of former days, with my father and uncle asking after our health and wanting to know everything about the work we'd been doing. Then the two of them would get to talking about a topic that had never come up back in Pyongyang: their old life in Japan. I remember one time, my sister and I listened, mouths agape, as our father recalled a competition he had won with carrier pigeons he himself had raised. He then lowered his voice and explained that in Japan you could say whatever you wanted in front of anyone without being scared and that you could find anything your heart desired, including pigeon food—as long, of course, as you had the means.

"That's not just a detail," grumbled my grandmother.

I don't remember anything bad being said about the North Korean regime or its leaders at any time during our first year of detention. My relatives found joy simply in evoking their childhood memories. Sometimes the two brothers would softly intone old Japanese melodies. Father loved to sing "A Song for My Mother" to my grandmother to thank her for all her attempts to cook us something edible. The song had to do with a loving mother who sits knitting gloves, her eyes made red by icy winds and want of sleep. The lyrics lacked a certain poetry, but they moved us and made the tears flow from Grandmother's eyes. She was the one who had originally dragged the family into this whole mess, but she was also the one who made it possible for us to resist. She made it possible with her care and encouragement and pluck. It's only thanks to her that I survived, and the same goes for my sister. The poor girl needed all the care and attention she could get. People are horrified when they hear how old I was when my family got taken to Yodok, but then I tell them about Mi-ho, who was only seven. I don't know if that child faced the same hardships I did in the camp; we almost never saw each other during the day, and at night she was as exhausted as everybody else and immediately collapsed into sleep. That was something else the camp stole from us—our sibling bond. I think about her now with great regret and affection. She survived because she was strong—very strong. For despite my grandmother's support, she ultimately was left to confront the snitches, the agents, the weariness, and the hunger all alone.

The spring of 1979 had arrived. It was my second spring in the camp, and it followed a winter that camp veterans counted as mild. Spring is a hard season for the detainees of Yodok, the worst, I believe. Many withstand the cold of winter only to perish in the season of rebirth. Children and the elderly are most afflicted. The prisoners often called it "the yellow season," because people felt out of shape and weak at the slightest physical exertion; they suffered from dizzy spells and in the most severe cases saw the sky as yellow instead of blue. Those who were unable to protect themselves in the preceding months died. The key was to take advantage of the fall, when fruit and vegetables could still be found, to consume like bears in hibernation, eating enough to get through winter and fight through spring. That's the most important thing I learned in school. I didn't learn it from my teachers, of course, but from fellow students, some of whom had already been in the camp for close to three years. They explained that to survive, one had to steal corn and soybeans, to do it methodically, systematically, eating as much as one could in the fall and stashing the rest against the harder times of the seasons to follow. There was no other way to survive.

Our corn rations were extremely meager: adults who worked from sunup to sundown had a daily allowance of 500 grams; others, including children, were allotted 400 grams. Vegetables were not distributed at all, and the few cabbages and turnips we managed to grow in our little plot were nowhere near enough to feed a household. Despite the risks of getting caught, we wound up stealing whatever we could get our hands on. We stole from the vegetable fields, from the agent's plots, from the cornfields. We also took advantage of logging expeditions to gather wild berries, which could only be found up in the mountain, since around the villages everything was picked clean. The detainees were like goats: they devoured everything. Whatever they didn't eat right away, they dried and ate in the winter; and when any kind of animal fell into their hands, they ate that, too.

Despite these precautions, more than a hundred people died in our village every year—out of a population of two to three thousand. Many former Japanese residents were interned in 1976 and 1977, the year of my arrival in the camp. That period and the months that immediately followed were among the most murderous I ever knew at Yodok. The newly arriving prisoners were usually the first to die. If you made it through the adjustment period, though, you could expect to live for a good ten years more. The most important thing was fighting malnutrition, which was more punishing than even mistreatment by guards. Most of the camp's diseases were not very serious, but in our weakened state a simple cold could kill. Psychological factors doubtless also played a role. Those who once lived in Japan were accustomed to a comfortable, modern existence and consequently suffered more than the others. For them, the adjustment to normal North Korean life had already been difficult enough. Many had hardly negotiated this transition when they suddenly found themselves transported to a concentration camp! The arrest itself was a brutal shock, a terrible blow to their spirit. These were people who pinned their every hope on Kim Il-sung and his brand of communism, and from one day to the next they saw themselves thrown into a camp, labeled traitors and sons of criminals, and treated as the lowest of slaves. It was more than many of them could take.

I almost died during my first months in the camp. The primary reason was the corn. Despite my grandmother's tireless efforts to make it appetizing, after a certain point I just couldn't digest it anymore. My problem was not in the least extraordinary: everyone struggled with it, though women for some reason had an easier time. I didn't know of a single man who didn't suffer at least one serious bout of diarrhea during his stay in Yodok. The ordeal, which generally lasted two or three months, would leave one thin and greatly weakened. The diarrhea was made all the worse by the ghastly conditions of the latrines. The filth was unspeakable. With the sparkling whiteness of our Pyongyang bathroom still fresh in my mind, just the sight of the small stinking huts was enough to make my stomach turn. There were only seven outhouses with four places each for an entire village of two to three thousand people. We did our business Turkish style, squatting over a tank we did our best not to dwell upon. No paper, of course. Each visitor had to come prepared with his own supply of sufficiently wide leaves. Bean and sesame leaves worked best. In July, during the rainy season, there was the danger of overflow; but it was much worse in winter, when the excrement froze and gradually built up toward the lip of the latrine. The detainees then were forced to choose between chiseling away at the growing mountain of excrement with a pickax or getting up in the middle of the night and digging a new hole of their own. If you chose the latter, it was worthwhile keeping track of the location, because you might later want to retrieve what you buried and use it to fertilize your vegetable bed.

Nineteen seventy-nine was probably even harder on my family than the preceding year. We'd faced the challenges of those fateful initial months, but weariness, malnutrition, and despair now nearly got the better of us. I was still friendless and often scorned by my teammates, who mistook my inability to keep pace for willful laziness. In the space of a few months or years, the camp had turned them into little savages. Several tried to provoke me and show me up, so that I would respect their would-be superiority. But having been in the camp since their early youth, they were all runts, and I didn't let them push me around.

My stomachaches, however, continued unabated. I could feel my strength dwindling, and my three or four daily fits of diarrhea were not helping. Just as grievous, though, was the absence of my mother, whom I missed more poignantly with every passing day. My grandmother had long been at a loss to explain her absence, but in that year, 1979, the explanation finally came. One day a security agent summoned my father and announced to him that his wife had requested, and received, her divorce. Father doubted the process had been voluntary, but it was impossible for him to know for sure. The uncertainty deepened his sadness and anxiety. As for me, I couldn't understand what it really meant. Grandmother—looking more haggard than I'd ever seen her—told me it meant that my mother would never come now and that it would be best for me to forget about her.

Despite her age, Mi-ho never faltered. She was always calm, even taciturn. An introvert, she never ceded to the temptation of outright rebellion and so she was never once beaten at school and only rarely punished with extra work. I didn't see much of her during our years in the camp, but I know she has a heart of gold. While everyone else I knew would leap on their food and devour it as quickly as possible, Mi-ho often gave up her share to someone she suspected might be hungrier. And yet she worked as hard as anyone. How I pitied her when she came home at night, shoulders bowed with exhaustion, her face downcast and dirty. I could do nothing for her. I could do nothing for any of us. Today Mi-ho lives in North Korea, and I still can't help her. She does appear in my dreams, though, where she is always running after me, but never with the anger and reproach that appear on my uncle's face during his nocturnal visitations.

When news came that we wouldn't be seeing our mother for a long time—and maybe never—I reacted less courageously than Mi-ho. I was devastated. I'd just turned twelve, and I remember wishing I would die soon. Everything became unbearable, and I no longer had the will to live. I was also very angry at my grandfather, believing he must have done something very bad to bring us so much misery. My grandmother tried to remind me what a good man he was and how much he loved me, but I was sure she was shielding me from his real crimes.

We got news of him only once, and that was a full three years after his disappearance. We discovered that he had been sent to Senghori, a camp some forty kilometers outside Pyongyang. Among people in the know, the prison was considered exceptionally brutal, but since it was located in a restricted military zone, hardly anyone among the general North Korean populace was aware of its existence. My grandfather had been sighted there by the father of a friend of mine, who was one of only a handful of men ever to survive that terrible place. His transfer to Yodok was a truly extraordinary event, but unfortunately, he had very little to tell me about my grandfather, beyond having seen him. Yet he did have quite a bit to relate about Senghori itself. He told me that its political prisoners were put to work in coal mines, where the pace and conditions were such that no one could hope to ever rejoin normal life—if such a thing can be said to exist in North Korea. He said several prisoners had once seen a group of fellow inmates exterminated. The witnesses were working on a mountain road when they were commanded to turn their backs while a truck passed. Disobeying orders, they watched as the truck stopped a little farther down the road. A group of prisoners were pulled out, lined up along a ditch, and shot. No one knew what they'd been accused of. Senghori ultimately was shut down after the publication of a report by Amnesty International that exposed the goings-on there. The existence of Yodok has also been criticized abroad, and I expect that camp number 15 will one day be as well known in Europe as it is in North Korea; but will the notoriety really help? While North Korean authorities would be happy to dispense with the bad publicity, the camp is too important, and holds too many people, to be closed or moved—unlike Senghori, which, though extremely severe, was considerably smaller.

Yongpyung, another hard-labor camp, is located within the Yodok complex itself. Its inmates are worked harder, locked up at night, and allotted less food. Located within Yodok's high-security zone—where the unredeemables are held—Yongpyung is the location of the rice paddies used to feed the guard population. Redeemable prisoners accused of committing some particularly egregious act could also be transferred to Yongpyung. This is what happened to the family of my friend Choe Myun-ho after his father bashed a guard's head in with a rock. A former top official in the Worker's Party, Choe's father was assigned to the gypsum quarry upon arriving at Yodok. It was a backbreaking, dangerous detail, on which laborers had to fill dozens of truckloads a day. His boy, Choe, was always being provoked and tormented by a particularly brutal guard infamous for whipping prisoners. When my friend's father saw him spit in his son's face, he became enraged and hit the guard over the head with a rock. The man collapsed and fell dead on the spot. The father was arrested and publicly executed at Kouep, one of Yodok's two public execution sites, after which his family was transferred to Yongpyung.

In the first months of 1980, a rare happy circumstance befell our family. My uncle was transferred to the camp's alcohol distillery. It was a major promotion and cause for the whole family to rejoice. Not only would my uncle be spared the grinding fatigue of farmwork, but by occasionally rerouting surplus inventory he could actually turn a little profit. The distillery jobs were among the most sought after in the camp. Work details in the gypsum quarry and the gold mine were reputedly the hardest and most dangerous. At the other end of the spectrum were the sweatshops, where my sister worked, and the farm produce shops, where the agents went to procure their cheese, bean curd, oil, and salt. (If the shops ever ran a surplus, the leftover foodstuffs were exported for sale outside the camp.) The coppersmith shop was also considered a good place to work, as was the joinery, where my father had been assigned to assist several seasoned craftsmen. But at the top of the list were the office jobs. We could imagine nothing better than sitting in an office, warm and sheltered from the winter cold. The lucky detainees selected for secretaryships were responsible for tracking major events: prisoner deaths and arrivals, the transport of goods in and out of the camp, the quantity of food distribution, and so forth. It was easy, human work, and it came with the assurance of shelter.

The agricultural teams like the one I was on could be occasionally pulled from the fields to help expedite a lagging production schedule elsewhere in the camp, or to lend a hand at the quarry. On a few occasions, I was temporarily assigned to work on construction sites, several of which were small dams. Every few months, camp authorities also trotted out their latest version of the "Let's Earn Some Dollars for Kim Il-sung" campaign. These crusades were intended to make us heave with enthusiasm at the idea of harvesting exotic hardwoods, gathering wild ginseng, or producing whatever else the Party thought might fetch a few dollars on the free and open market.

But to return to the distillery. It produced three distinct types of brandy. The first two, distilled from corn and acorns, respectively, were intended for export and sale. The third, which counted snake as one of its ingredients, was reserved exclusively for the pleasure of our local guards. Before being added to the stew, the snakes were starved to death over a period of one month, which caused their venom to lose its toxicity. As far as I can recall, this spirit had no official name. Around the camp, we called it either *Yodok Soul* (literally, "Yodok Alcohol"), snake brandy, or *Byungbung Soul*, after the 5,000-foot-high mountain that is the native habitat for a rare medicinal plant sold as far away as Japan. The prisoners at Yodok always spoke with great confidence about the exceptional quality of the camp's snake brandy, though I doubt any of them ever tasted it. The only prisoners who were ever admitted into the distillery were people who couldn't or wouldn't drink. In my ten years in the camp, I never saw a single prisoner drink so much as a drop of the local specialty.

My uncle was the distillery's technical chief for seven years. No one had ever held the position for that long, and only the handful of detainees who worked in the guards' office or in the bachelors' kitchen ever enjoyed as many privileges. To land such a job, a prisoner needed to win the protection of a guard, which is what my uncle somehow managed to do. His ascent had begun with the unpleasant surprise of being called on to serve as an informant. My uncle was not overjoyed at the prospect but was afraid to refuse. He also knew that if his reports were sufficiently useless, he would be cut loose from the duty in no time anyway. As it turned out, my uncle's reports were not bad, though, just innocuous. This avocation earned him a few packs of cigarettes and some extra food, but more importantly it gave him the chance to befriend a guard, whose good word later helped him get the job in the distillery. My uncle's degrees in biochemistry, which gave him a competence in matters of distillation, no doubt also influenced the authorities' decision. After becoming lord of the alcohol bottles, my uncle wielded enormous power and prestige in the camp, though his position was mined with countless dangers and intrigues. Security agents were always dropping by to ask for a bottle on the sly, which left my uncle with a very dubious choice. If he refused their request, the agents had no shortage of ways to exact their revenge; if he relented, he could run into serious trouble during the next production audit.

His work also came under the daily supervision of a security agent who was assigned to the distillery, a man not likely to forgive irregularities. My uncle had to play it slick, fulfilling his substantial clandestine distribution while making everything appear on the up and up. Pressured by a number of different guards—some of whom were rivals—my uncle had plenty to keep him up at night. One day he was called before a camp official who wanted him to admit he'd given alcohol to a colleague who ran the distillery. My uncle firmly denied the charges, guessing correctly that the interrogation stood on little but rumors and suspicions. The official wasn't so easily put off, however, and at one point he suggested the sweatbox might help stir my uncle's memory. The thought was almost enough to make him confess, except that a confession would land him in the sweatbox all the faster—and as a confirmed criminal, rather than a mere suspect. Moreover, the guards compromised by his confession would become his sworn enemies and make him pay for their troubles. He would also risk a transfer to Senghori or to one of the other camps of no return. So he kept his mouth shut. Toward 3:00 A.M., the tone of the interrogation changed. The official suddenly stood up, perfectly calm, and led him out of the office. Outside, he turned to my uncle and said, "Your silence is appreciated. Keep it up!"

The sweatbox is one of the harshest punishments imaginable, and since it could be used as retribution for the most trifling of offenses— offenses that would seem downright ridiculous on the outside— it was perpetually dangling over our heads. I exaggerate when I say "our heads": it wasn't used on kids. But when a relative was sent to the sweatbox, the whole family was scared, not knowing whether the loved one would make it out alive. Stealing three ears of corn, responding to a guard's command with insufficient zeal, missing a role call, even if the absence clearly had no wrongful intent—any of these was reason enough for being sent to the sweatbox. Yet all were "faults" that anyone could commit—and often had to commit—to survive.

The sweatbox was located by the guard shack near the main entrance to the camp. The sweatbox was also a kind of shack, but much smaller than the guard's and devoid of any openings. The way survivors described it—I was lucky enough never to suffer that torture—recalled the prison cell of Henry Carrère, a.k.a. Papillon. The box is shrouded in total darkness and its occupant is given so little to eat that he will devour anything that comes within arms' reach, which is most often a wayward cockroach or centipede.

Among the prisoners I met in the camp was a celebrated former athlete who made a name for himself in Yodok by making it through a very long stint in the sweatbox. According to rumor, his survival secret was to eat every insect he could get his hands on. Whether or not true, it won him the nickname Cockroach. Park Seung-jin, as he was really named, had lived his earlier moment of glory back in the 1966 World Cup in England. That year, the North Korean team on which he played miraculously made it to the final round, where in the first game it managed a 1–0 victory against the mighty Italians. To celebrate their victory, the players went on a wild drinking binge and, by the end of the night, were seen carrying on in public with some girls. By the next game day—two days later—they still hadn't fully recovered. The team nevertheless got off to a strong start, taking an early 3–0 lead against the Portuguese. But then they fell apart, and Portugal stormed back to win the game 5–3.

In Pyongyang, the national team's barroom antics were judged bourgeois, reactionary, corrupted by imperialism and bad ideas. Upon arriving back in Korea, the whole team—save for Park Dou-ik, who, suffering from stomach pains on the night of the party, had been forced to stay in his hotel room—was sent to the camps. Unfortunately for Park Seung-jin, his celebrity won him few favors in Yodok, as he discovered when he was caught stealing nails and cement from the camp's construction materials shop where he worked. He denied all wrongdoing and lashed out at the accusing guard. His punishment was a three-month stint in the sweatbox, which he somehow miraculously survived. By the time I arrived at Yodok, he'd already been there almost twelve years. And he was still there when I left the camp, though by then he was much weakened.

The sweatbox breaks even the sturdiest of constitutions. It is possible to survive it, but the cost is often crippling and the aftereffects are almost always permanent. It is simply grisly: the privation of food; close confinement, crouching on one's knees, hands on thighs, unable to move. The prisoner's rear end presses into his heels so unrelentingly that the buttocks turns solid black with bruising. Hardly anyone exited the sweatbox on his own two feet. If the prisoner needed to relieve himself, he raised his left hand; if he was sick, he raised his right. No other gestures were allowed. No other movements. No words. If the watchman pacing back and forth in front of the sweatbox failed to notice the raised hand, well, that was too bad. The prisoner continued to wait in silence. If he talked, he was beaten; if he moved, he was beaten. And if it was not a beating he got, it was a special punishment: he was made to crouch over the septic pit for half an hour, with his hands behind his back and his nose bowed downward. In the realm of horror, only punitive forced labor withstands comparison to the sweatbox. In a way, the two are equal and opposite. With forced labor, one has to move without stopping, excavate mountains of earth, lift massive logs into the back of trucks—all at an infernal pace. If nothing useful needs doing, a useless task will work just as well: digging a hole or a trench, for example, then filling it right back up. According to the Yodok veterans, the one appreciable difference between punitive forced labor and the sweatbox was that the latter automatically added five years to one's detention.

아홉

DEATH AT YODOK

Our schoolwork continued on, as numbingly boring as ever. Disinterest, fear of beatings, and physical weariness collaborated to make dunces of us all. And assignments such as "summarize the Great Leader's speech of July 3, 1954, and learn it by heart" were not the thing to awaken our intellectual curiosity. Then again, that was never the point. As long as we looked like we were paying attention, the teachers were content to let us sit and do nothing in peace.

We didn't have that option in the afternoon, however, when the outdoor work was hard and demanded all our attention. To ensure that our minds and muscles stayed alert, our hoeing and weeding was supervised by armed guards, who could impose physical punishment if a production quota went unmet. Sometimes the guards' attention slipped, but most of the time they kept us working like animals. I worked so hard I mostly had neither time nor energy enough to miss my mother—or even think of her. And yet I know her absence had a lot to do with the gloom I felt gradually enveloping my existence.

I found no more comfort returning to our hut at night. The atmosphere around our bowls of corn was so dreary and bleak. We seemed beaten, drained, wrung of all hope. It wasn't anyone in particular, it was the entire family that was going through a rough patch. Grandmother—always the most loquacious of the brood—lamented her fate openly and blamed herself for the family's misfortunes. She also talked a lot about Grandfather and with time grew ever more indignant that he was being punished because of some meaningless Party intrigue.

"Why not me?" she kept asking. "Why was he condemned and not me?"

According to some of our fellow prisoners, my grandfather had been arrested as part of a larger sting operation, which had nothing directly to do with either his remarks about the country's inefficiencies or his general penchant for unwanted frankness. What his arrest apparently had sprung from was the Han Duk-su affair, the power struggle that raged for a time within the Chosen Soren's political leadership in Japan.* Many of the former Japanese residents living in Korea had also weighed in on the conflict, both directly and indirectly. Grandmother, acting with her usual verve, had been among those in the fray, but Grandfather hardly took an interest. "Politics was never his thing," my grandmother kept saying. "But it's still him they got." I think she would have been content to take his place. She could never avoid feeling responsible for the family's imprisonment and her husband's condemnation. Poor woman. She had given everything she had to communism. For fifteen or sixteen years she militated for its ideas, believing she was realizing them in her beloved homeland. And this same country had taken away the man she loved and sent her and her family to a camp. She felt so guilty that she couldn't stop asking for our forgiveness. Yet it was the lamentation

---

*See page 120.

and regrets—coming from a woman who was once so indomitable and strong—that really shook us to our core.

During this dark period, my uncle first confessed to having attempted suicide. It had happened during his first week in the camp, before the rest of the family's arrival. I remember my grandmother listening to his story in complete silence and then just sitting there for the longest time, looking stunned and broken. When she snapped out of it, she stared straight into my uncle's eyes and pronounced the following with a depth and solemnity that admitted no contradiction: "If anyone should die first here, it's me, not you, but me. Don't ever start up with that again." Unsure whether she had succeeded in convincing him, she followed with another argument—or a cry, rather—asking, "How could I live if you died?"

My uncle tried to end it all again the following year. This time along with my father. When I got home from work my grandmother told me the two of them had gone up to the mountains with the intention of hanging themselves from a tree. I started to shake uncontrollably, then threw myself on my mat and thought about them as hard as I could, muttering, "Come back, come back." I don't know how long I had been this way when I heard the shack door creak open. It was them! I cried from happiness. They had thought themselves ready to depart the camp at any cost, to leave the hunger, the humiliation, the filth, the thrashings. In the end, the only thing that had stopped them was knowing their suicide would bring trouble upon the family.

Suicide was not uncommon in the camp. A number of our neighbors took that road out of Yodok. They usually left behind letters criticizing the regime, or at the very least its Security Force. They were heedless acts which virtually guaranteed that the letter writer's family would be sent to a place worse still than Yodok. Truth be told, some form of punishment would await the family regardless of whether or not a critical note were left behind. It was a rule that admitted no exceptions. The Party saw suicide as an attempt to escape its grasp, and if the individual who had tried the trick wasn't around to pay for it, someone else needed to be found. Some suicides tried to palliate the punishment their relatives faced by leaving behind notes in which they maintained their innocence but reiterated their faith in communism and in the regime of the much-beloved Great Leader. This sometimes induced the agents to treat the surviving family with relative leniency and merely add five extra years to the family's original sentence, whose length they, in any case, never knew.

After my father and uncle emerged from their bout of depression, it was their turn to give moral support to my grandmother, who was teetering ever more precipitously between anger and desperation. They now tried to ply her with the very arguments she had recently used on them: there was still a chance they would get out one day; the family needed to stick together; they were like a five-man team, where the fate of each member depended on the fate of the group as a whole.

We did, indeed, stick together, and while Grandmother was never to recover her former joy for life, she did regain her equilibrium. At the same time, her political thinking also gradually began to change. When we first arrived at the camp, she had wanted to believe that our internment stemmed from a judicial error that the authorities might soon set aright. As time passed, however, her attention shifted to the camp itself, which she contended served no purpose in a Communist regime. If opponents and protestors were unhappy in North Korea, it was enough simply to kick them out. Running a camp such as Yodok was a crime, a concentration of inhumanity. Eventually, she went still further, asserting that though North Korea still wore the badge of communism, it had lost its soul. I think it was only then that she truly realized she'd been had. With the years, she stopped bemoaning her fate and beating herself up about it; but her criticisms didn't stop, they just metastasized into anger and hate. She now saw the regime as closer to Hitler's world than anything Marx or Lenin had envisioned. True communism she would never renounce, not even now that its actualization no longer seemed within easy reach.

Grandmother was also the first among us to fall seriously ill. She came down with a disease called pellagra, which was once common among North American Indians and caused by a diet too rich in corn. The malady was not difficult to diagnose. The sufferers' skin turned rough, their nails fell off, and their eyes became ringed with deep wrinkles that made them look as if they were wearing glasses. The prisoners at Yodok called pellagra the "glasses disease" or the "dog disease," because eating dog was a guaranteed antidote— though I suspect any meat would have done. If victims couldn't get meat, they started losing their senses and trying to eat anything they could get their hands on. Sometimes this actually made them better, but many died from the disease.

In the spring of 1981, I was assigned to help bury the bodies of prisoners who had perished during the previous winter, when the frost-hardened earth had made timely interment difficult. As with any detail, the work was carried out after school; but since it was considered somewhat unusual, we were rewarded with a few noodles to supplement our ration of corn. This would have sufficed to make interring bodies a desirable detail, but the work offered another very practical advantage. The burial team could strip the corpse of its last remaining clothes and either reuse them or barter them for other essentials. But the fringe benefits came at a price. Since Korean tradition requires that people be buried on a height, we had to carry the bodies up a mountain or to the top of a hill. We naturally preferred the hills at the center of the camp to the steep mountain slopes near Yodok's perimeter. Their proximity allowed us to follow tradition without traversing tens of kilometers. But the neighboring hills eventually became overcrowded with corpses, and one day the authorities announced we would no longer be allowed to bury our dead there.

We thought the order had been given for health reasons, but we soon found out how wrong we were. I was walking back to the village with my team one evening after a day of gathering herbs up in the mountains, when we were overtaken by a terrible stench. As we walked on, the odor grew stronger and stronger until we finally came upon the cause. There were the guards, bulldozing the top of the hill where we'd buried so many of our dead. They actually dared to set upon corpses! They didn't even fear disturbing the souls of the dead. An act of sacrilege held no weight for them compared to the possibility of growing a little more corn. As the machines tore up the soil, scraps of human flesh reemerged from the final resting place; arms and legs and feet, some still stockinged, rolled in waves before the bulldozer. I was terrified. One of my friends vomited. Then we ran away, our noses tucked in our sleeves, trying to avoid the ghastly scent of flesh and putrefaction. The guards then hollowed out a ditch and ordered a few detainees to toss in all the corpses and body parts that were visible on the surface. Three or four days later the freshly plowed field lay ready for a new crop of corn. I knew several people from my village who were assigned to plant and weed it. Apparently, it was horrific work. Since only the larger remains had been disposed of during the initial cleanup, the field-workers were constantly coming upon various body parts. Oddly enough, the corn grew well on the plot for several years running.

That scene frightens me more today than it did back then. At the time, I remained relatively calm before that spectacle of horrors, which is perhaps the most telling indication of just how desensitized I had become. The more I witnessed such atrocities and rubbed shoulders with death, the more I desired to stay alive, no matter the cost. Maybe I didn't have it in me to become a snitch or turn on my friends, but I had lost much of my capacity to feel pity and compassion. I developed a savage will to live and a disregard for everyone around me. I also learned to control my emotions in front of the guards, which was very much in my self-interest. Trickery had come to play an ever larger role in my life. I used it to procure food, catch rats, steal corn, fake work while doing nothing, and get along with the snitches.

I wasn't alone. A few weeks after the bulldozer incident, I came across a group of people from my village standing around a woman who was loudly weeping and venting her sorrows about something. As I joined the crowd, I gathered she was lamenting the death of a relative, whose body was apparently still in the family hut. "Ah, why did you die so quickly?" she kept saying. "Why did you depart this cursed world?" The unhappy woman must not have noticed that a well-known snitch was in the crowd, as well as the leader of one of the work brigades. Her son, who was also there, saw the danger and tried desperately to catch her eye. It took him a while, but he finally did it, at which point the mother did a complete turnabout. "Oh," she continued without the slightest transition, "why did you leave this world, which had become so happy under the wise governance of our Great Leader?" No one dared to laugh, but after that, neither could anyone cry.

My bouts of diarrhea finally abated thanks to an opium-based remedy procured by my uncle, most likely in exchange for a bottle of alcohol. But spring 1981, like the previous spring, was bringing more than its share of corpses. This was the season of the most oppressive agricultural labor, when we toiled without pause, hoes and spades constantly in hand. Most of the tools were in a sorry state, and when there weren't enough to go around, the guards ordered unequipped prisoners to turn the soil with their bare hands.

The work did have one benefit, though it usually came too late to help the weakest among us. In the fields, it was sometimes possible for us to catch frogs, which were plentiful in this season. The amphibians could be skinned and cooked fresh or set out to dry in the sun and used later. Their eggs were also very much in demand. Besides the frogs, we also ate salamanders that we caught near a sweet-water spring. I never much liked the way they tasted, but they were said to be very nutritious. Eating three a day was supposed to keep you in great shape, like vitamin concentrates, though I have no idea whether this was science or faith. The way to eat a salamander is to grab it by the tail and swallow it in one quick gulp—before it can discharge a foul-tasting liquid. I often brought my grandmother salamanders so that she would stay healthy, but she never got the knack of swallowing them whole. We kids were the only ones who could do it easily. We ate anything that moved, making even the undiscriminating adults look picky by comparison. By the time a group of prisoners finished working a field, no animal was left alive. Even earthworms were fair game. When we were done with her, nature always needed a couple of seasons to recuperate before she could provide a fresh bounty of food. And yet our hunger remained, piercing, draining.

TEN

THE MUCH-COVETED
RABBITS

I changed jobs many times that year. None was easy, but in the monotonous life of a child prisoner any change is welcome. I worked in the cornfield, buried corpses, gathered herbs up in the mountains. The outdoor work saved me from developing full-blown pellagra, whose first symptoms—the infamous glasses and the mad desire to eat everything—I had begun to develop. Up in the mountains I caught frogs and boiled their eggs in water, and this helped me fight off the disease.

For several weeks I also filled in at the gold mine, located on the lower slopes of the camp's northern hills. Toward the end of the Japanese occupation, the mine had been assessed insufficiently profitable and shut down. Now that there was a free labor force, however, the calculations had changed. Seven to eight hundred men were employed in the mine. Working in teams of five, as in the rest of the camp, they entered the shafts without any protective gear—not even so much as a hard hat—and with only a flashlight or candle-powered storm lantern to light their way.

One day we learned that a special mobilization had been decreed to augment national gold production and to help raise foreign currency for Kim Il-sung. To fill the new quotas, the guards transferred several agricultural teams over to the mining site. My team was one of them, though we were spared the difficult details in the farthest depths of the mine. That, fortunately, would have required additional training, something that was considered a waste of time during a mobilization period. My team's work consisted mainly of gathering and transporting minerals extracted by the veteran miners. While my job was relatively safe, I was very much affected by the scariness of the place. All of the galleries, even the deepest ones, which ran down a hundred yards, were poorly shored up. Cave-ins were common and left many miners permanently crippled. The place was so frightening it was considered cursed. According to camp legend, it always drew lightning during storms and, according to a few old-timers, several people—among them one guard—had been struck dead there by lightning bolts.

The mine work was as exhausting as it was dangerous. Since we didn't have wheelbarrows, we were left to transport the excavated dirt on our backs, in sacks that we then dumped into oxcarts at the mouth of the tunnel. From there the gold-bearing earth was wheeled to a water basin, where other prisoners would pan it for nuggets. Since the river that wound through the camp was also believed to bear gold dust, during the mobilization period, special teams were formed and made to stand in the water and pan that, too.

Despite the dangers, mining did have a few advantages. To compensate for the difficult working conditions, miners were given slightly more food and sometimes even a little oil. Since the guards

didn't dare descend into the shafts, the miners were also left in relative peace with no one around to insult and bark orders at them.
The snitches were still around, however, and their presence was
enough to maintain discipline and guarantee a steady output. To
avoid being punished with an extra night shift, the miners had to
keep moving from six in the morning until noon, and then again
from one in the afternoon until seven or eight in the evening.

My tenure in the mines marked a new stage in my life at the camp;
it made me realize there were others even less fortunate. At least I
didn't have to spend all of my days in the subterranean dust and
darkness. I had also triumphed over the "yellow spring," pellagra,
and even my interminable diarrhea. Finally, I had gotten to know
the internal workings of the camp and discovered how to pull the
strings necessary for survival. I learned how the work routine func-
tioned and how assignments were organized; I figured out the
guards' system for reshuffling work teams, changing orders and
standards, and assigning team leaders. When a special campaign
was launched, I was prepared for it, knowing I had nothing to fear
from these punctual mobilizations that would end in a week or two,
at which point I would rejoin my family.

I also understood the camp's system of indirect supervision,
which made the work team, rather than the guards, the primary
means of surveillance. The official security agents only kept a close
eye on the newest arrivals—to break them in, mostly. Once prisoners were established the guards tended to keep their distance during the day, reasserting themselves in the evening, when it came
time to tally the day's production. That's when they really got tense.
If our quota wasn't filled, we were supposed to keep working until
it was, but since the guards would have to stay out in the cold, too,

and wait to get home to their families, they sometimes overlooked the shortfalls. Recognizing this made me feel a lot less powerless. In short, I'd made it through the adaptation period that, depending on the detainee, could last anywhere from several months to several years. I was twelve years old now, and I no longer wanted to die. I even started to develop that sixth sense all prisoners have for sniffing out informants. While I now realize they were just as much victims of the system as I was, back then I thought of them as agents of voluntary evil.

A few months after my arrival, a kid who was part of my gang was selected to be an informant. The moment he got the news he came to tell us about it, warning, in jest, that we'd better start watching what we said around him. Unfortunately, we couldn't help but take him at his word. We grew more suspicious of him by the day. Whenever he was around, we refrained from criticizing the guards and teachers and refused to complain about work. The unhappy child became increasingly isolated from the group and was eventually pushed out altogether. His situation was truly perverse, and ultimately it provided him all the motivation he needed to become a genuine snitch.

Living under constant threat of denunciation, my friends and I came to hate these spies with a passion. We held them in contempt and always tried to get them back for their treachery, no matter what honor might be due their age or former station in life. Our classmate was only twelve years old, but Cho Byung-il was in his sixties—a ripe, almost biblical age by camp standards, and one ordinarily worthy of respect. A former cadre of the Korean Communist Party in Japan, he'd become one the camp's most dreaded informants. Many prisoners had him to thank for extra work details; his snitching had even sent several people to the sweatbox. While he was hated by all the prisoners at Yodok, it was the children who despised him most. His bald head and round face were the targets of countless taunts and jeers. One day, as we were passing in front of the soybean-processing shop where he worked, he tried to peek out at us and eavesdrop on our conversation. When we saw his head appear in the shop window like a rising moon, we nearly split our sides laughing. For a long time after that, just mentioning that scene was enough to make us crack up. I'm sure Cho Byung-il felt miserable about his social and physical decline. He suffered from malnutrition just like the rest of us and, eventually, from incontinence, too, a disability the camp's hospital made no attempt to treat. In the end, his death was as ghastly as it was miserable. He had always lived by himself, apart from the other bachelors. One day, some prisoners who had suffered from his informing locked him into his hut and left him to die of hunger. The authorities knew what was happening, but did nothing. Cho Byung-il had grown too old and weak to be of use.

I remember another informant at Yodok whose specialty was snitching on kids. Once, we decided to exact our revenge by setting a trap for him at a spot he crossed several times a day. There, we dug a hole resembling the fugitive trap we had once discovered up in the mountains. In place of sharpened stakes, we filled the ditch with excrement from the latrines. The trick seemed easy and risk free. As luck had it, the infamous Wild Boar came along first and wound up burying his foot ankle-deep in feces. We saw the whole thing from our little hiding place, and now had every reason to try to keep our location secret; but our teacher was so outraged and was having such a hard time extricating himself from the mess that we just couldn't restrain ourselves. We started laughing so hard we cried. Within a minute he had us collared and was giving us the thrashing of a lifetime. When he was done, he ordered us to scoop out all the excrement by hand and carry it over to the neighboring garden plots, where it would serve as fertilizer for the guards' summer vegetables. The abominable chore took days, during which time several of us saw our hands break out in strange-looking pimples and blisters.

Fortunately, that fall the Wild Boar was temporarily transferred to another camp and replaced by the only teacher I had at Yodok whom I still remember fondly. Thanks to this man, my life at Yodok took another turn for the better.

Shortly after his arrival, he called me into the teachers' hut and kindly began asking me a series of questions: What was my name, why was I at Yodok, when had I arrived? and so forth. Then he asked me how long it had been since I'd last had a sweet.

"Not since I've been here," I answered.

"Would you like one?" he asked. And with that, he handed me a piece of candy, which I immediately stuffed into my mouth. As I sucked, he told me not to mention it to the others.

In class, he spoke in a normal tone of voice and called us by our first names. Unaccustomed to such treatment, we were on our guard at first, despite the happiness we felt at finally having a teacher who behaved humanly. He stayed on in the camp for only a year or a year and a half, but it was his confidence and protection that led to my being selected warrener.

As in every school in North Korea, save in the capital, the students at Yodok had the responsibility of raising rabbits. This had nothing to do with teaching us about anatomy or rodent physiology, nor was it a matter of inculcating students into a love of animals or nature. The animals were raised to provide skins for the army's winter coats. Each class had about two hundred rabbits, which were tended to by student guards of the class's choosing. Rabbits were serious business in North Korea, and bringing up a quality pack could make a teacher's reputation. Each wanted to present the most beautiful rabbits and the largest litters, so as to provide the army with the greatest number of skins. One teacher at Yodok even tacitly encouraged us to steal corn for "our" rabbits, so they would be the best-fed nest in the school.

The position of rabbit guard was desirable for the simple reason that it replaced one's afternoon work detail. The job consisted mostly of cleaning the cages twice a week, which was easy because trays under the cages caught all the droppings. (The cages were built this way in order to protect the delicate health of the rabbits, whose feet must never remain too long in the damp.) When the other students went out to gather grass for the rabbits, I was supposed to weigh their harvest and report it to the teacher. Some of the gatherers were girls whom I liked, so when they came back a few pounds short, I just closed my eyes and jotted down the requisite 70 pounds. I also had to maintain the fires in the guardhouse adjacent to the school and in the special room dedicated to the study of Kim Il-sung's revolution. We and our parents could damn well freeze to death, but Kim Il-sung's relics, posters, and pictures needed always to stay warm.

Another, more difficult, part of the job was protecting the rabbits from rats that tried to squeeze into the cages at night to devour the young. To try to control the problem, we set up rat traps using wooden boxes, but the captured rats very often chewed their way out. The only viable solution was to mount a guard. The late hours were hard on kids who were only twelve or thirteen years old, but it gave us a chance to steal a few fruits and vegetables from the fields otherwise reserved for the guards. The rabbits were our allies in these endeavors, disposing of the pits and peels that threatened to denounce our thieving. Thanks to them, I was able to taste melon for the first time in three or four years.

Given how hungry we were, it was inevitable that our stealing would eventually get out of hand. The armed sentinel who guarded the vegetable field always fell asleep in the first hours of his watch. The temptation was just too great. While we were never caught red-handed, the pillaging eventually became conspicuous, and our teacher let us know that we, the students, were the leading suspects. He quoted the loss estimates and threatened serious consequences should the trend continue. We were in a tight spot and needed to weigh our options carefully. Apart from the teacher's warnings, we also had to consider another, more immediate danger. A new guard had been assigned the night watch, and he was likely to be less sleepy and quicker on the draw than his predecessor. Yet if the theft ended from one night to the next, it would be tantamount to admitting our guilt— with God only knows what consequences. We ultimately decided we should keep on stealing for a while, making the best we could of the moonless nights and the aural cover of what turned out to be the new guard's snoring. In the end, it was so easy we almost felt sorry for the guard, who was always getting chewed out by his superior.

We slaughtered the rabbits in the fall, stripping and preparing the furs in their most luxuriant season. As for the meat, its dispensation was the exclusive prerogative of the agents and their families, who each received their own rabbit. When they came to fetch their animals, we waited on them like regular butchers, asking if they wanted their animals eviscerated; whole or cut into pieces; with or without the head, liver, or kidneys. What joy we felt when they turned up their noses at the lungs or the heart and bade us, "Keep it!"

Yet it wasn't just disgust that compelled the guards to refuse the offal; in Korean culture there is the idea—born partly of generosity and partly of disdain—that one should always leave a portion of what one eats to an inferior. It's a way of establishing one's superiority, of saying, "I don't need it" and "it's good enough for you but not for me." To break with this custom is to lose face, even in a camp, and this was very much to our benefit. At the end of the slaughter day, we divvied up the innards and cooked them in the simplest and fastest way possible, by boiling them in water. It seemed like the most exquisite meal ever, though the kids were sometimes so hungry they couldn't wait for the meat to cook and just ate it raw.

Such charmed days were painfully rare, however, and pinching a rabbit on the sly was no easy feat. The animals were continually being counted and recounted, so that even a single disappearance would be immediately noticed. A short while after the departure of my favorite teacher, I was nevertheless able to pull off the trick a couple of times. Though I had been relieved of my post as rabbit guard some time before, I still knew the system by heart: the layout of the rabbit area, the duration of the rounds, the habits of the various personnel. My chance came on a night when my work team was being punished for missing a lumber quota and kept late to finish the job. The shortfall hadn't been our fault. The work site was a long way from the village, making it impossible for us to go home for lunch and get the energy we needed to complete the job. When night fell, we sneaked into a nearby field and stole some corn, but rather than satisfy our hunger it only whet it. Then someone suggested we steal a rabbit, which everyone thought was a great idea. I swear I could see my cohorts' eyes glistening in anticipation. I was chosen for the mission, along with two friends—Hwang Yong-soo and Bae Jong-chol—who kept the lookout while I slipped into the warren. Within a few minutes, a rabbit had been pulled from its cage, killed, skinned, eviscerated, and its intestines buried. Our only fear now was that the smell of cooking might give us away. So while the rest of us went back to work, one member of our gang cooked the rabbit at a safe distance. It was one of the most delicious dinners I ever had. It had been six months since I had so much as tasted meat. I still think about that night sometimes, wishing I could see those kids again. The last time I saw them was when they left the camp. Hwang was the first to go, then me, then Bae. And that was it, silence. . . . They probably remember that night, too, and shake their heads thinking about the huge risk we had taken. With North Korea ravaged by famine, they may even regret not being back in Yodok, within reach of the rabbit cage.

If I were to improve my nutritional intake and realize my dream of becoming the family's provider of meat, the better option was rat. One of my coworkers—a camp veteran—was the first to introduce me to the dish, going so far as to demonstrate its proper preparation. Despite my revulsion, I couldn't resist the odor of grilled meat—which was not deceptive, because the rat was truly delicious. Though the rodents were everywhere, trapping them was difficult, especially because most were quite small. The other challenge was figuring out how to reuse the traps, since the first captured rat left behind a smell that warded off the others. After much experimentation, I discovered that the smell could be eliminated by passing the contraption over a fire. By this time, however, I was already perfecting my newest trap design, which used wires strung across the entrance of the rats' nest to snare and strangle the animals as they tried to exit. My clever little invention was completed in 1982, and thanks to its increased catch, I was able to supplement the family's small food ration.

Mi-ho made less fuss about eating her first grilled rat than I did. True, I initially lied to her about the nature of the meat, but when I later told her the truth she wasn't the least bit disgusted. The poor girl was so hungry. She was suffering from pellagra, and that dish may have been her last shot at survival. At my urging, the entire family eventually took to eating rat. My uncle was the hardest to convince, but after a few months of demurring, the day came when his hunger pains were just too sharp and he, too, relented. That was the last time I saw him turn down a piece of grilled rat meat. The Yodok rats, it should be said, were fine specimens—much finer than any rat I ever caught in Seoul—and since they reproduced quickly, they were the only food product in the camp that was never in short supply.

I was not the only prisoner in Yodok to hunt rats. There were many devotees of the sport, and each had his or her own technique for trapping and preserving the game. I discovered that a friend of mine had turned his hut into a full-blown breeding ground. The other kids and I had noticed that he was always in good shape, while we, despite our little supplements, remained hungry and thin. Was he stealing food? Was someone giving it to him? Fearing that we had begun to suspect him of collaborating with the guards, the boy called us over to his hut one day for an explanation. His family was allotted two rooms, just like we were, but instead of using all their living space, they all squeezed into one room and left the second space entirely for the rats. To attract them, my friend had stolen corn from the fields and spread it on the floor. The plan worked perfectly, and the number of nests multiplied. The only maintenance required was sprinkling a little corn on the floor every few days. Whenever he got hungry, all my friend had to do was grab a wire trap and fish out a rat. It was a veritable pantry, the secret to his robust health.

Another of the camp's rat hunters prospered by taking advantage of his job as the watchman of the corn depot. The vast corn storage area, which was surrounded by barbed wire, contained about a hundred small wire-mesh silos, into which the prisoners emptied their harvest at the end of each day. Prisoners were allowed to enter the area freely, but the guard always patted them down on their way out. Everyone envied the guard's job, especially because the man who held the position was chubby—indeed almost fat—which only helped fuel speculation about his diet. People said that he always had meat in his mess tin. While most prisoners were sure he was doubling as a snitch, they also suspected him of stealing corn. Security eventually got wind of the rumor and sent guards to search the man's hovel. What they discovered was a large receptacle packed tight with salt-cured rat meat. The guards couldn't be more pleased with the man's ingenuity and fervor in controlling the population of the corn-thieving rats. The complaints of his libelers only helped shore up his position.

All the meals and extra rations provided me by the rats gradually changed my view of these animals. I began to see them as useful, even precious, on a par with chickens and rabbits. I was truly grateful for their existence, and still am. Absurd though it may seem to those who have never known hunger, I actually felt a connection with them. I remember an encounter I had with a rat in our hut one night. Raising my head from my mattress I saw him staring at me from between two floorboards. We were locked in each other's gaze, staring into each other's eyes for what seemed a long time, until the spell broke and he scurried away. Before entering the camp, I had thought of rats as scary and disgusting. Today I think of them as touchingly kind animals.

Sentiments aside, the following winter was a hard one, and the occasional rats I trapped afforded considerable succor. The snowfalls were so heavy that only the sharpest crags of the surrounding mountains broke through the thick blanket of white. It seemed as though nature were telling us that to get out of Yodok we would have to be the world's greatest mountain climbers—a title none of us could claim.

As long as the temperature remained above −13°F, work went on as usual. Imagine us kids, dressed all in rags, trying to chop down a tree whose essential oils were needed for the latest "Let's Earn Some Dollars for Kim Il-sung" campaign. With our bodies waist-deep in snow, we had to dig evacuation paths in case a tree didn't fall as planned. Many adults were killed and maimed that way. Once a tree was down, we chopped off its branches and hauled the trunk to the foot of the mountain on our shoulders. At the end of the day, we returned to our huts—my, I almost said homes!—with our hands and feet frozen stiff and our whole bodies utterly exhausted.

On one particularly cold winter's day, I got home with a strange, painful stinging sensation in my feet. I tried soaking them in lukewarm water, but this only made them feel worse. Cold water was the only thing that brought relief. The next morning when I woke up, my toenails were solid black and I was unable to walk. The guards let me work inside that day, weaving wicker baskets as I had been taught in school. My toenails eventually fell off, but I miraculously escaped necrosis and the amputation it would have necessitated.

New shoes were given to us every two years, but the quality was so poor, and our work so demanding, that the pair never lasted more than a year. To avoid frostbite, we wrapped our extremities in layers of rags and dried rat skins. In the bitterest cold, we swathed our heads and faces in tattered castoffs, leaving only our eyes uncovered. Such measures could never contend with the bitter −10°F temperatures that descended on the mountain. The only way to keep from freezing was to keep moving; but this wasn't something everyone could do, and every year, several old people died from the cold.

These memories come back to me whenever I go skiing and see high, snow-covered mountains with sheer black crags. I try to explain my feelings to South Korean friends, but have little success. Where they see an ideal landscape, I see the natural barriers of Yodok, a place conceived for human misery, whose gloom still has the power to overwhelm me.

열하나

ELEVEN

MADNESS STALKS
THE PRISONERS

In the summer of 1982, my situation improved further. I finally made a friend. The camp had received two new prisoners, space aliens practically, whose extraordinary clothes and looks reminded us of our lost world. They were an elegant woman with dark glasses and her handsomely attired son, whose delicate white skin contrasted invidiously with our own, which the sun, wind, and snow had tanned into leather. Our jaws dropped when we saw them.

Within a few months their finely cut clothes would lose all their charm. The woman stopped wearing her glasses; she and her son looked just like everybody else in the camp. Less than a year after their incarceration, the boy, whose name was Yi Sae-bong, fell seriously ill and couldn't move his legs. Fortunately his paralysis didn't last. At first we had a hard time communicating, because having grown up in Japan, he only knew a few words of Korean; but he learned the language quickly and was soon able to tell me how he arrived in Yodok. He was a little older than I was and his family had lived in Kyoto, the city with the most powerful Chosen Soren cell outside the homeland. When the Party leadership in Pyongyang chose Han Duk-su to head the Japanese wing, the Kyoto cell protested. Han Duk-su, they said, was being parachuted in; he had never done anything for the struggle in Japan. The opponents backed down when they learned Kim Il-sung himself was backing the controversial nomination, but by this time the Great Leader's embittered candidate was determined to exact revenge. Many members of the Kyoto cell wound up in the camps. They had opposed the will of Han Duk-su and, by extension, that of Kim Il-sung, and this was a crime that could not be easily forgiven.

Like so many who hadn't understood the danger, Yi Sae-bong's father decided to move his family back to North Korea. He planned to come first, then send for his wife, three sons, and daughter. Shortly after arriving, however, he was arrested for espionage and sent to a hard-labor camp. When weeks passed without a word, Yi Sae-bong and his mother came to North Korea to try to find out what had become of him. Instead of receiving information, they were arrested and sent to Yodok.

I loved to hear Yi Sae-bong's stories about Japan. I was amazed by all its brands of beer—imported from all over the world—and by the huge black American soldiers that walked the streets. My imagination soared at the mention of France, England, Germany, and Czechoslovakia—the latter inspiring particular wonder. What most sparked my interest were the thick, juicy steaks people ate with a knife and fork. I wanted to know how they were cooked, what they were garnished with, the side dishes that accompanied them. I was sad I couldn't imagine the taste of catsup and offended by the rampant wastefulness, which included the lighthearted dumping of half-eaten meals. More shocking was my friend's contention that grocers sold fruits the whole year round. I was almost ready to suspect him of lying. It was either that or believe that Japan really was a paradise—a possibility that, despite my father and uncle's warm recollections, I still found difficult to admit.

Yi Sae-bong was the person who really introduced me to Japan. I hassled him constantly for details about his school, the traffic, the movies, the department stores. I was amazed at his description of the automobile assembly lines, where robots put entire cars together in a matter of minutes. The most astounding things, though, were the toilets: they had chairs where you could sit and read a paper, or have a cup of coffee. It seemed so incredible to me. The first time Yi Sae-bong went to the bathroom at Yodok, he threw up.

The winter of 1982–83 was relatively mild. Yet ice and snow, alas, were not the only causes of death at Yodok. There were also accidents—terrible accidents—such as the one I witnessed while on special assignment at the clay quarry. A group of children had been ordered to excavate a ton of fine earth in a single afternoon, an absurd quota. Working without the benefit of either adult supervision or scaffolding, they burrowed child-sized tunnels into the foot of the cliff, whose environs soon turned gloomy with shadows and dust. My job that day was to carry the excavated earth over to the trucks that hauled it away. I was just finishing one of my trips when I heard a muted rumble, then screams. I ran toward the tunnel. There had been a cave-in. A number of kids were trapped. As I worked furiously to help dig out the rubble, I overheard my schoolmaster bantering with one of the guards.

"What a piece of work, these kids!" he mused. "Gone and col-lapsed the cliff again. What idiots! Guess they won't be siring any little ones!"

We managed to pull five or six of the kids out alive, but all the rest were dead. I remember their bodies, blue but not yet stiffened. I felt a terrible anguish. These kids were my age; fate had simply been less kind to them. They should never have been given that work. Unfortunately, the story doesn't end there. After giving the crew a sharp dressing-down, the teacher ordered everyone back to work—for the sake of discipline, I suppose. Still shaken, the kids begged to have the job put off until the next day, but the teacher wouldn't have any of it. He kicked and slapped them until they rejoined their post—at the very place where they had just extracted their friends, whose bodies lay within view, waiting to be moved to the camp's hospital.

Every village had one hospital—supposing that term may be justi-fiably applied to a two-room office reeking of disinfectant. This was the place where it was decided whether or not a prisoner was fit to work. The hospital's furniture consisted of a table, a few chairs, and a single worn-out bed. The doctor, who was a prisoner, didn't even have a lab coat. His only medical instrument was a stethoscope. There was a nurse to assist him, but he had no medicine apart from a few anti-inflammatories. The doctor's main duty was filling out exemption forms for sick prisoners so they wouldn't have to attend role call. In exceptionally grave cases, the doctor sometimes obtained antibiotics or some other injections, but this was rare.

Patients requiring immediate surgery—appendicitis cases, for example, and amputations—were treated at the camp's one real hospital, otherwise reserved for guards and their families. It was a place prisoners tried to avoid, because after surgery they would be left alone, often to develop deadly secondary infections. If a patient required more than a rudimentary operation, he went untreated and was left to die.

Prisoners who suffered from pulmonary and hepatic ailments—of which there were many—were quarantined in a permanent structure. Epidemics, especially of flea-borne diseases such as scabies and typhus, were common. I had a teacher who was so afraid of contracting a disease that he once ordered us to leave the classroom and not come back until we had stripped completely naked, picked all the fleas off our bodies, and crushed them with our fingernails. Whenever a case of typhoid fever was discovered, the sufferer was immediately transferred to a quarantine area and his entire village put under strict isolation. The village residents were then sent up into the mountains until the end of the disease's incubation period. After that, the village was burned to the ground and rebuilt by the survivors.

The quarantine area was divided into two wards, one for contagious patients, the other for psychiatric cases. In neither ward was medicine ever available. The patients simply waited for their illness to pass. If they died, that was just too bad. If they made it, they were sent back to work. The camp had many cases of madness, which put both the patients and their families at great risk. A mad person could say just about anything. If it was favorable to Kim Il-sung, nothing bad happened to the patient's relatives. If, however, the comments were inappropriate, the patient and his family could pay with their lives. Madness struck young and old alike, the newly arrived and the veterans, as the climate of terror, scant food, and insufficient sleep put us all perpetually on the edge of delirium. Unbalanced prisoners had to work like everybody else, only their rations were made proportional to the amount of work they performed. If they worked a little, they had little to eat. If they didn't work at all, they starved to death.

I saw many fits of madness at the camp. One student had to leave school for a month after a severe beating by his teacher left him delirious. Another instance of madness happened to a good friend of mine, whose father had been Kim Il-sung's history teacher as well as the national minister of education. The boy's family arrived at the camp the same time we had, and he and I were in the same class. One day in the middle of a lesson he suddenly started raving, then stopped and broke into uncontrollable laughter. When I asked him what was so funny, he told me that the previous day his brother had given him something very delicious to eat. He glanced about with a strange look in his eye and made nonsensical replies to all our questions. Finally, the teacher sent him home. We didn't see him again for six months. Then he was back, apparently sane, only more reserved and taciturn than we had previously known him to be.

열둘

TWELVE

BIWEEKLY CRITICISM
AND SELF-CRITICISM

In 1984, I turned fifteen. I was a scrawny kid, even by camp standards, but I had more stamina than most prisoners my age. I could walk briskly for hours with a heavy load, having come a long way since the time I passed out from carrying a log. No matter how much healthier the newly arrived kids may have looked, none could keep up with me. At Yodok, habit, training, and trickery counted more than strength. Arriving at the camp at the age I did left me plenty of time to develop these qualities.

My stamina gradually won me the respect of my fellow prisoners. Even the guards—who weren't exactly the accommodating type— never exerted extra effort to treat me like a "troublemaker" or make my life miserable.

So do I dare admit it? Some mysterious bond had come to attach me to that place. I've heard it said that the most miserable slave is one who is content with his fate. That wasn't my case; I wasn't content. But Yodok was the big cage where I'd grown into adulthood and wised up to life's tough realities. It was my cage—and though I was a hungry prisoner, draped in rags, I had learned to love the scents wafted by the springtime breeze, the tender green of the season's first leaves, the last glow of pink in the evening sky as the sun sank behind the mountains. I could never look at those mountains, where I was sent to gather wild ginseng and other medicines with my friends, without being moved: I would recall the time we accidentally came nose to nose with a bear and had to hightail it down the mountain; the meal we made of a captured snake; the sweetness of the wild berries we picked. These were precious memories, of friendship and solidarity. These things were rare in Yodok, and I held them close. They gave me strength, unlike the old memories, whose return saddened me and sapped my strength. I hadn't renounced the memory of my aquariums, but I now thought of them as belonging to another world, the abandoned world of Pyongyang; of my grandfather, who was condemned for being a "criminal"; of my mother, whom they'd kept back and forced to divorce my father; of Japan, as it had come alive in the stories of my uncle and father. This past had no place in my new life, which could accommodate no softheartedness, mine or anybody else's.

That's how I gradually grew into adulthood, though as far as the camp was concerned, the transition happened all at once, with "The Last Class."* Our teacher had a pithy way of illustrating what

---

*Kang Chol-hwan is alluding to a short story by Alphonse Daudet entitled "La Dernière Class," which appears in the collection *Contes du lundi*. The story tells of a painful falling out between a class of Alsatian students and their French teacher, whom the students abruptly abandon in favor of a newly arrived German *Lehrer*. Koreans lived through a similar experience during Japanese colonization, which explains why this story is one of the most famous works of French literature in Korea.

that transition really meant: "Up to now," he told us on the last day of school, "when you made a mistake, even a serious one, no one shot you for it. But from here on out, you're responsible adults, and you could get shot. Consider yourselves warned." While waiting for a death sentence to test the full extent of my new responsibility, the very next day I was allowed to taste the simple joys of adult life in Yodok: physical labor from morning until night, distended quotas, the occasional distribution of third-quality tobacco, public criticism and self-criticism sessions, and so forth.

Criticism and self-criticism sessions were nothing new to me. Such meetings took place in every North Korean school, Yodok's included. But outside the camp, these ideological exercises tended to be peaceable and rather formal in nature. Nothing much happened if you didn't criticize well enough or happened to criticize too sharply. At Yodok, the stakes were much higher. Punishments consisted of hours of nighttime wood chopping, even for ten- and thirteen-year-old children.

The atmosphere was strained. You could feel the fear and hatred spreading through the room. The kids were not as adept at controlling their emotions as adults, who knew that the wisest thing to do was accept whatever criticism they received. The adults understood that it was just a routine that had nothing to do with what their fellow prisoners really thought of them. Soon enough, the criticized person would have to criticize his criticizer. Those were the rules; there was nothing personal about it. Yet the faultfinding of peers was hard for kids to accept, especially if it struck them as unfair. They would get angry, argue, interrupt each other. While the short Wednesday meetings, which lasted only twenty minutes, were hardly long enough to cause major damage, the Saturday afternoon sessions, which went on for nearly two hours, were considerably more lively and tension-filled. A special session also could be called if something unusual took place in school. The substance of adults' criticisms was basically the same as the children's: "I wasn't careful enough during work hours . . . I arrived late yesterday because I was being careless, etc. . . . ." The major difference was that the children's sessions were conducted among one's classmates.

As for the adults, each work team had its own location for Wednesday sessions, while on Saturday the different teams met together in a single large building, on whose walls hung the portraits of Kim Il-sung and Kim Jong-il. At the far end of the room was a platform with a table where the prisoner sat to present his self-criticism. Next to the table stood two guards, along with a representative of the prisoners. There were no other chairs in the room. The other prisoners sat on the floor in groups of five, clustered with their fellow team members. The assembly hall was always overcrowded. Some prisoners dozed off, others became nauseous from the intensity of the body odor that hung in the air—there was no soap at Yodok.

Sometimes we met in smaller groups to prepare our Saturday presentation in advance. Four of us would discuss our misdeeds for the week, while the fifth team member took notes. Afterward, the report was presented to a camp administrator, who selected the week's ten most "interesting" cases for presentation before the entire village. The prelude to the ceremony varied somewhat, but the main action was always the same. The wrongdoer would step onto the platform, his head bowed, and launch into his self-criticism with a fool-proof formula such as, "Our Great Leader commanded us," or "Our Dear Leader has taught us." The offender then cited one of the head of state's great "Thoughts," relating either to culture, youth, work, or study, depending on the offense committed. A typical criticism went something like this:

"At the famous conference of March 28, 1949, our Great Leader stated that our youth must always be the most energetic in the world, in terms both of work and study. But instead of heeding the wise reflections of our respected comrade Kim Il-sung, I twice arrived late at role call. I alone was responsible for this tardiness, which demonstrated neglect for the luminous reflection of our Great Leader. From now on, I will wake up a half hour earlier and make myself equal to the task of fulfilling his orders. I will renew myself and become a faithful warrior in the revolution of Kim Il-sung and Kim Jong-il."

Then it was up to the presiding security agent to decide whether the self-criticism had been satisfactory. If it had been, the prisoner could proceed to the next step: criticizing someone else. If his criticism was found wanting, the agent would ask a member of the audience to expand on the criticism proffered. If the accused tried to defend himself, a third prisoner, and, if necessary, a fourth, was selected to take up the assault. Self-defense was never wise, because the review couldn't end until the prisoner admitted his faults. Once a prisoner relented, we moved on to the next preselected case. The session lasted from an hour and a half to two hours, running from 9:00 P.M. until about 11:00 P.M., which wasn't always enough time to get through all ten cases. If time ran short, the agents consolidated the wrongdoing of an entire team, or several of its members, into a single presentation. A member of the guilty team would then present the self-criticism on behalf of everyone involved.

The sessions were so conventional and formalized that it was hard to take them seriously—despite the perfect silence imposed by the hard gaze of the guards. We were like bored kids in a class they find meaningless. The smallest distraction would set us off. It happened several times that audience members let out an audible fart in the middle of a self-criticism. A little nothing like that was all it took to shatter the ceremony's contrived solemnity and send the guards into a fit of rage. Sometimes they pretended not to hear, but other times they demanded to know who the culprit was. "Who farted?" they screamed. "The person who farted stand up!" If no one confessed, the guards kept us seated there until the criminal was identified, which eventually he always was. The prisoner would then be pushed toward the self-criticism table to expiate his fart with a mea culpa, at the end of which he usually received a week's worth of supplementary work details.

We dreaded these long meetings that shortened our nights need-lessly. They were too much of a sham to ever take seriously, but that's not the way camp authorities saw it. They were always reminding us that "work alone can't root out your rotten ideology. You need control." What they meant was ideological control, and maintaining it was in part our responsibility. Hence, on arriving at adulthood, we were given three notebooks in which to trace the development of our ideological healing: "The Politics of the Party Notebook," "The Revolutionary History of Kim Il-sung and Kim Jong-il Notebook," and the "Life Assessment Notebook." All three accompanied us to the criticism sessions, so we could jot down all the lessons we learned.

To help advance our edification and reeducation, we also attended two classes a week to learn revolutionary songs and deepen our understanding of the life and thoughts of Kim Il-sung. The curriculum (called "the teachings") consisted largely of lis-tening to articles read out loud from the *Rodong Sinmun* newspa-per, of which three copies arrived weekly at the supply office. We weren't allowed to read the paper ourselves, because the direct word of the Party was reserved for security agents. Reprobates that we were, it would have been dangerous to expose us to more than a few preselected articles, and even these needed to be interpreted for us by the agents. With our rotten ideology, we were quite capable of misunderstanding their true intent. To say "interpreted" really gives the agents too much credit. All they ever did was pound us over the head with the Great Leader's most tired platitudes. "I read you this article because the Americans and their puppets in Seoul are once again threatening war. The imperialists' appetite for conquest threatens the peace, and to withstand it we must be ideologically armed."

I don't know whether the guards believed everything they said, but when they raised the possibility of a new war, some of us got nervous. We had always been told that if "the imperialists and their lackeys" ever invaded North Korea, the camp's personnel would kill us before the enemy arrived. I still had hopes of leaving Yodok one day. I had no desire to be shot by guards without having the pleasure of seeing them run for their lives. These sorts of threats sent a chill up my spine, but they made very little impression on the older veterans. *Whatever Will Be, Will Be* was their motto, and whatever happened outside the camp was of no interest to them.

Still under the rubric of our ideological reeducation, the agents sometimes tested our allegiance to Kim Il-sung by making us sing endless verses of "The Song of General Kim Il-sung." Part of the song goes, "In North Korea a new spring is everywhere on its way." "*Pang-bang kok-kok*" means "everywhere, without exception." I remember one old prisoner in the camp who had emigrated from Japan, like my parents, and who spoke Korean with a heavy accent. Instead of singing "*pang-bang kok-kok*," he accidentally used a slightly different semantic form—"*yogi chogi*," four syllables that mean "scattered in disorder" that have a rather negative association with filth and trash. The people who heard his slip began to laugh so hard they cried. As a consequence, he was criticized and labeled an "ideological deviant" and was almost sent to the sweatbox.

At the beginning of every year, we had the privilege of having Kim Il-sung's extended New Year's address read to us. The speech was the focal point of a two-day event featuring an absurd recitation contest. It could have been worse, though. It was January—a time when the thermometer often dipped well below 0°F—and instead of being outside, we were gathered in a well-heated room. On the first day, we transcribed the speech in one of our notebooks, while the guards walked around to make sure we were making an effort. The next day, we worked on memorizing the speech by heart. The biggest challenge was figuring out how to doze off without being caught. The guards really only expected us to study the Great Leader's message and to regurgitate a few quotes. To keep us honest, they picked a handful of prisoners to recite what they had learned. The top three contestants won prizes—considerable ones, given our condition. The winner got a coat, the runner-up, a pair of socks, and the second runner-up, a pair of gloves. The kids' recitation contests were held in class, with the winner receiving a short reprieve from the usual work schedule.

My memory of these speeches has blurred somewhat, but I remember that they always started with an account of the previous year's accomplishments in agriculture, industry, the armed forces, and so forth, and ended with a list of "goals for the future." Somewhere in the middle came a nod to the Koreans residing in Japan, who under the clairvoyant leadership of Han Duk-su were continuing to lead a courageous battle in the heart of enemy land. There was also the inevitable mention of the South Koreans, who were suffering a cruel separation from the motherland and toiling under the yoke of America's lackeys.

Many other leaders' birthdays were important enough to serve as a pretext for pedagogic celebrations or breaks from the normal routine. On such days, candy was dispensed to all the kids in the country, sometimes even to those in the camps. I remember Kim Il-sung's seventieth birthday in 1982. As soon as I got my candy, I ran home to show it to my grandmother. By this time, her faith in the Worker's Party was long gone. "Ah, yes," she said. "We gave them everything we had, and in return we get years in the camp and a few cheap candies. There's something to celebrate, my child. And a big thank you to Kim Il-sung!" I ate the gifts anyway. They were the first goodies I'd tasted in a very long time.

The other birthdays were less solemn events, occasioning the dispensation of more modest rewards, but they were greatly appreciated. On January 1 (New Year's Day), February 16 (Kim Jong-il's birthday), September 9 (anniversary of North Korea's declaration of statehood), and October 10 (anniversary of the Party's founding), we would gather to watch an edifying television program or a revolutionary film. We were let off work early to see the screening, but sometimes we were so tired, we immediately fell asleep.

I remember one movie about the life of Kim Il-sung in which the main actor looked just like the Great Leader himself. He was taking his troops through the vast Manchurian plain, frozen solid by cold and snow. The fierce struggle of Kim Il-sung's partisans and the cruel treatment meted out to them by the Japanese were supposed to arouse our sympathy, but they wound up doing the opposite. We were struggling as hard at Yodok as Kim Il-sung's partisans in the frozen plain; what we saw on the screen was parallel to our own condition. The dungeons, brutalities, inhumane guards, and meager food supplies depicted on the screen didn't move us; we were living with these things every day. Except our misery wasn't inflicted by enemies but by our own compatriots!

I remember another film about a man named Kapyong, who signs up to be an auxiliary in the Japanese army. There wasn't a kid in the country, Yodok included, who hadn't seen the movie at least a dozen times and knew every word by heart. In the movie, Kapyong goes to work for the Japanese out of necessity and from a lack of political consciousness. Then he meets Kim Il-sung, sees the light, and is transfigured into a true patriot. He then sings a lament about the humiliations he has suffered at the hands of "Fascists." In the theaters back in Pyongyang, all the kids would sing along with it. At Yodok we did the same thing, except that during the refrain, instead of bemoaning the fate of "poor Kapyong," everyone substituted their own names.

The propaganda was so grotesque, the teaching method so crude, we were bound to reject it. Like every education institution in North Korea, the camp's school had a room dedicated to the study of Kim Il-sung's revolution. On one wall hung a huge portrait of the Great Leader, and everywhere you looked were photos illustrating the different stages in his heroic life. It was forbidden for anyone to enter the room with bare or dirty feet. We had to wear socks—and not just any socks. For this occasion we had to put on the special pair given to us on Kim Il-sung's birthday, the pair reserved for visiting the holy sites. What did it matter that we suffered from the cold in winter and waded in puddles during the rainy season with only rags around our feet? Wearing Kim Il-sung's socks for such workaday purposes would have been a sacrilege. The Party's code of conduct required that we reserve them for the Kim Il-sung annex, no matter how much we needed them in our daily lives.

One day I came to school having forgotten that the Wild Boar had scheduled a visit to the Kim Il-sung room. I was wearing my ordinary socks, which were full of holes and barely holding together after half a dozen darnings by my grandmother. I was panic-stricken, especially when the Wild Boar asked everyone who "accidentally" forgot their socks to raise their hands. Fortunately, I wasn't alone. Two-thirds of the class had their hands up. The teacher was outraged. He ordered the scatterbrains to go outside and line up. Then he came out and kicked his way furiously along the row of children. He was wearing canvas army boots and let them fly with all his strength. During beatings, it was common for us to exaggerate our pain in order to win sympathy, but this time we had no room for exaggeration. The cries of pain were real. The blow I took to the stomach was so violent that I collapsed on the spot and lost consciousness for a half hour.

A couple of years was all it took for the camp to utterly change a child. Instead of turning us into stalwart admirers of our Great Leader's regime, as it was intended to do, the camp taught us how to rebel, jeer, and mock anything vaguely whiffing of authority. Within a year or two of arriving, a prisoner lost every scintilla of respect he might have had for the Party. Our disdain spread like gangrene, beginning with the guards, then slowly, inexorably, making its way up to the great leaders.

I think the camp also changed me psychologically. As a child I was outgoing and restless. When people meet me today, they find me reserved and somewhat distant. Growing up in the camp made me shut myself off from the world. I learned about suffering and hunger, violence and murder. For a long time I was angry at my grandfather. Only around 1983 did I begin to realize that not he but rather Kim Il-sung and his regime were the real causes of my suffering. They were the ones responsible for the camp and for filling it with innocent people. All during my childhood, Kim Il-sung had been like a god to me. A few years in the camp cured me of my faith. My fellow prisoners and I were the wayward sheep of the revolution, and the Party's way of bringing us back into the fold was to exploit us unto death. The propaganda, which exalted North Korea as the people's corner of paradise, now struck me as revolting.

THIRTEEN

PUBLIC EXECUTIONS AND
POSTMORTEM STONINGS

Having reached majority—as defined in the camp—I was obliged to begin attending a ceremony I would have preferred to skip. Yet few things were optional at Yodok, least of all the things that were most awful. Many public executions had taken place over the preceding years of my internment, but as a child I was not allowed to see them. Two of my more curious friends had once sneaked into an execution and described it to me afterward. The story left me feeling hollow and disgusted, which is the way my father and uncle always looked when they came home from one of these events, their faces hard and unnatural. They would skip their dinner and just sit there, never saying a word about what they had seen. If I pressed, they just shook their heads, and observed that "Yodok is no place for human beings."

The first public execution I saw was of a prisoner who had attempted to escape. We were dismissed from work early that afternoon so we could attend the execution. The whole village was there. The skies were rainy and gray—as I always remember them being on execution days. The event took place at a spot called Ipsok, a beautiful little elbow on the river, which turned into an island during the heavy rains. *Ipsok* means "large elevated boulder," which is exactly what the spot was: an enormous rock, as big around as a house, standing by the shore.

Three desks were set up for the occasion: for the head of the camp, the village chief, and the military guards. As the prisoners arrived they took their seats on the ground in front of the desks. Farther off, a small truck was parked under a tree. I was told that that was where they were keeping the condemned man. I felt anxious. The older veterans sat chatting. A few wondered aloud about who the man might be. Most talked about other things. Several prisoners used the time to gather herbs. Attending a few executions was all it took to render the experience perfectly banal.

Finally, the head of the camp stood up to read the condemned man's resume. "The Party was willing to forgive this criminal. It gave him the chance here at Yodok to right himself. He chose to betray the Party's trust, and for that he merits execution." During the silence that followed, we could hear the condemned man scream his final imprecations in the truck. "You bastards! I'm innocent!" Then suddenly his cries stopped. We saw two agents pull him down from the truck, each holding an arm. It must have been ages since he had last eaten. All skin and bones, it looked as if he were being floated along by the guards. As he passed in front of the prisoners, some shut their eyes. Others lowered their heads out of respect. A few of the prisoners, especially the younger ones, stared widely at the barely human figure, hardly able to believe their eyes. The unhappy being who walked to his death seemed no longer a member of the family of man. It would have been easy to mistake him for an animal, with his wild hair, his bruises, his crusts of dried blood, his bulging eyes. Then I suddenly noticed his mouth. So that's how they shut him up. They had stuffed it full of rocks. The guards were now tying him to a post with three pieces of rope: at eye level, around the chest, and at the waist. As they withdrew, the commanding officer took his place beside the firing squad. "Aim at the traitor of the Fatherland . . . Fire!" The custom was to shoot three salvos from a distance of five yards. The first salvo cut the topmost cords, killing the condemned man and causing his head to fall forward. The second salvo cut the chords around his chest and bent him forward further. The third salvo released his last tether, allowing the man's body to drop into the pit in front of him, his tomb. This simplified the burial.

That unfortunately wasn't the worst spectacle that I beheld at Yodok. In the fall of 1986, a condemned prisoner who didn't have enough pebbles stuffed into his mouth, or had somehow managed to spit them out, began proclaiming his innocence and screaming that Kim Il-sung was a "little dog"—one of the worst things you can call someone in Korean. To shut him up, one of the guards grabbed a big rock and shoved it into the man's mouth, breaking his teeth and turning his face into a bloody mess.

In October 1985, two prisoners were executed by hanging. The victims were members of an elite military unit that had succeeded in fleeing the country. They were well trained and very familiar with the terrain. One of them got as far as Dandong, China, at the mouth of the Yalu River, before he was stopped by Chinese security forces and sent back to North Korea. The Korean authorities had searched for them everywhere, even in the camp. For two weeks, Yodok's prisoners were mobilized in the effort and forced to scour the camp grounds every afternoon. In our heart of hearts, we were grateful to the fugitives for the work-free afternoons. We thought of them as heroes. Their escape had accomplished the unimaginable. All of us were rooting for them and hoping they might tell the world about what was happening at Yodok. But it was not to be.

It wasn't until we were called to Ipsok one morning that we learned they had been caught. Adding to our surprise were the gallows that had been erected in place of the usual execution posts. Our two heroes were brought forward with their heads sheathed in white hoods. The guards led them up to the scaffold and slipped nooses around their necks. The first fugitive was nothing short of skeletal, but the second one, the one who had gotten as far as Dandong, looked like he still had some reserves of energy. Yet he was quicker to die. The other one clung to life, wriggling at the end of his rope like some crazed animal. It was a horrible sight. Urine started trickling down both their pants. I had the strange feeling of being swallowed up in a world where the earth and sky had changed places.

Once both men were finally dead, the two or three thousand prisoners in attendance were instructed to each pick up a stone and hurl it at the corpses while yelling, "Down with the traitors of the people!" We did as we were told, but our disgust was written all over our faces. Most of us closed our eyes, or lowered our heads, to avoid seeing the mutilated bodies oozing with black-red blood. Some of the newer prisoners—most of them recently arrived from Japan—were so disgusted they couldn't cast their stones. Other inmates, seeing an opportunity to rise in the estimation of camp officials, chose especially large rocks, which they hurled hard at the corpses' heads. The skin on the victims' faces eventually came undone and nothing remained of their clothing but a few bloody shreds. By the time my turn came, stones were heaped at the foot of the gallows. The corpses were kept dangling on the ropes all through the night, guarded by security agents, who made sure no one would try to bury them. To keep warm, the sentinels built a fire, which still smoked in the morning as crows began circling above the lifeless bodies. It was a ghastly scene. Awful.

Whose decision had it been to replace the firing squad with the gallows? The agony of hanging seemed terribly long—and the stoning ceremony was simply bestial. Yet the horror it produced was not unintended. The authorities wanted us to cringe at the very thought of escape—just as they longed to exact revenge against the fugitives who had briefly evaded their grasp. When the manhunt was still on, they had offered a reward to whomever found the fugitives first. They had sent their agents out with orders not to come back empty-handed. Once the fugitives were captured, the guards, who had suffered many threats and great physical weariness because of the escape, were ready to make the condemned men pay.

I attended some fifteen executions during my time in Yodok. With the exception of the man who was caught stealing 650 pounds of corn, they were all for attempted escape. No matter how many executions I saw, I was never able to get used to them, was never calm enough to gather herbs while waiting for the show to begin. I don't blame the prisoners who unaffectedly went about their business. People who are hungry don't have the heart to think about others. Sometimes they can't even care for their own family. Hunger quashes man's will to help his fellow man. I've seen fathers steal food from their own children's lunchboxes. As they scarf down the corn, they have only one overpowering desire: to placate, if even for just one moment, that feeling of insufferable need.

Ceding to hunger, acting like an animal: these are things anyone is capable of, professor, worker, and peasant alike. I saw for myself how little these distinctions mattered, how thoroughly hunger alters one's reason. A person dying of hunger will grab a rat and eat it without hesitation. Yet as soon as he begins to regain his strength, his dignity returns, and he thinks to himself, I'm a human being. How could I have descended so low? This high-mindedness never lasts long. The hunger inevitably comes back to gnaw at him again, and he's off to set another trap. Even when my grandmother was suffering from pellagra, the thought of bringing her soup only crossed my mind after I devoured a few rabbit heads. What leftovers I did bring her, she pounced on with avidity, searching furiously for any remaining shreds of meat. Only after she had eaten her fill did she stop to ask whether I had eaten. Once she was cured of the disease, she became her old self again, stoically mastering her hunger while preparing the family meals.

Our family's victory over death gave us new courage to face together the camp's shortage of food and surplus of suspicion and hate. At Yodok, however, pity and compassion rarely extended beyond the family circle into that world peopled with vicious guards and snitches intent on betrayal. When my work team was ordered to bury the body of a widely despised informant, we all began to curse under our breath. Carry that son of a bitch? No way! As far as we were concerned, he could rot right where he was. But the guards threatened punishment, and we had no choice but to haul him up the mountain. With each step we became more enraged at the thought of giving this man a decent burial. Intent on getting it over with as quickly as possible, we dug an undersized hole, then folded the cadaver and stomped it with our feet to make it fit. What a picture we must have made, five gleeful kids kicking a cadaver into its grave. He had comported himself like a dog, and he deserved to be buried like a filthy beast. Yet what about us? What had become of us?

The death of compassion was responsible for worse acts than this. I saw fathers, released from the camps with their bodies broken and depleted, turned out of their children's homes, hungry mouths with nothing left to give. Sometimes the fathers were left by the side of the road to die of hunger. Only their demise could bring any good, by clearing the way for the family's possible rehabilitation. The system seemed specifically designed to stamp out the last vestiges of generosity.

I thought I would never be rid of my hatred for the cruelest guards and informants, and that I would never let go of my desire for revenge. But when I finally got out of the camp, all I wanted was to throw out my memories like a dirty shirt. That was just me, though. There were people whose hatred never abated—people like Kim Song-chi. The only thing that sustained him through his imprisonment was his desire for revenge. In the old days, he had been a Party cadre in Japan. He was a big, beautiful man, with a deadpan sense of humor and sex appeal that had caused numerous scandals over the years. He had entered the camp in 1974 at age fifty-five and survived fifteen years there—a rare achievement for someone without a family. Always discreet, he was meticulous about not bothering others and had a rule about never asking anything of anyone. He had an exceptional ability to master his hunger, and I never once saw him wolf down a meal. He was still at the camp when I got out, but a little later I heard that he had been released. On rejoining the outside world, he discovered that his wife had divorced him and found a new husband and that his children had forsaken him as an enemy of the people. This only redoubled his desire for revenge. At the camp, he was nicknamed the Count of Monte Cristo, and he now demonstrated just how worthy he was of that title. He tracked down and assassinated the security agents who had arrested him and then, the rumor went, killed himself.

Toward the end of 1985, my family had a new and very serious cause for concern. My uncle the chemist, whose work in the distillation plant was a source of much benefit to the family, fell precipitously from his pedestal. Had vengeance been the cause? Was someone trying to remind him he was still just a no-good criminal? Whatever the reason, one day he was moved to the camp's hard-labor zone. As punishments went at Yodok, this was perhaps the worst, and few survived it. The work was conceived solely for the purpose of driving prisoners to their graves. Under close armed surveillance, my uncle was forced to toil without respite from morning until night. The work took place in a remote part of the camp; indeed, so remote that my uncle didn't even have time to return to his hut at night, but instead had to get his three or four hours of sleep on-site. Three months was the longest we had ever heard of anyone surviving under these conditions. My uncle made it through exactly forty-five days, when an agent, whose alcohol trafficking my uncle had kept faithfully concealed, intervened on his behalf and got him out.

열넷

LOVE AT YODOK

Sexual relations were forbidden in Yodok. If a couple was caught having sex, the man was sent to the sweatbox. The same rule applied to any guard who used his power to take advantage of a female prisoner. If he made it out of the box alive, he was transferred to another camp. Women were spared the sweatbox. Their punishment was public humiliation; they were made to stand before the entire population of the village and recount their frolics. Their stories were never graphic enough to satisfy the guards, who demanded a detailed description of the caresses the woman used and the way her lover responded to them. They wanted to know what the couple had done with their hands and tongues and what positions they had tried. Nervous laughter could often be heard from the kids in the audience. This was our version of sex education, and it came with a heavy dose of voyeurism. Our feelings were ambiguous, both ardent and embarrassed. The ecstatic faces of the guards, full of joy and violent threat, the woman's look of ravishment and humiliation, the snickering of the crowd: together they made for a rather sinister tableau.

A Myong-chul, a former camp guard who escaped to the South, has talked about the barbarous punishments he saw inflicted on women found guilty of sexual relations. There was a pregnant woman who was bound to a tree and flogged, another who had her breasts cut off, a third who died after being raped with a spade handle. I myself only had knowledge of the public confessions.

Sexual relations were banned in Yodok because they threatened to give life to a further generation of counterrevolutionaries. The North Korean state believes in eugenics, that people of undesirable origins should disappear, or at the very least be prevented from reproducing. I once saw an agent force a pregnant woman to disrobe and expose her rounded stomach to a crowd of assembled prisoners, then begin to beat and insult her.

"You, a counterrevolutionary, dare to bring a child into this world?" he screamed with fists flying. "You, from a family of traitors of the fatherland? It's unspeakable!"

The unlucky women whose pregnancies were noticed were usually forced to abort. A prisoner in the camp—a former doctor—was responsible for the procedures. The conditions under which they were performed, without anesthesia or proper surgical instruments, were chilling. A few women were able to camouflage their state and bring their pregnancy to term, but this made little difference in the end. The guards took the babies away as soon as they were born, and they would never be seen again. There were two women in Yodok who succeeded in saving their babies. One, whose pregnancy was discovered very late, simply refused to hand over her newborn. With everyone looking on, she told the guards they could kill her if they wanted, but she wouldn't give up her baby. She said they had no right to kill a child, who had never committed any crime.

"It would be treason against the Constitution of the Popular Democratic Republic," she cried. "If our Great Leader heard of this he would be very unhappy." She also said she intended to marry the father and make the child legitimate. To our amazement, the guards hesitated and then left her with her baby.

I remember her well because she was the older sister of one of my friends. Her father was a Worker's Party cadre in Japan and among the most faithful of Kim Il-sung's followers. Japanese police had once arrested him for hanging the flag of the Korean Republic on the facade of Kyoto's City Hall. After moving to Korea, he refused to accept gifts sent to him by friends in capitalist Japan. This man, who was Red to the bone, was nevertheless arrested, denounced as a spy, and imprisoned along with the rest of his family.

His daughter was amazingly robust: I saw her work the fields with more vigor than most men; but love works in mysterious ways. She had fallen in love with a guard, and when her pregnancy was discovered, the father confessed his crime and was sent to the sweatbox. Thanks to the rats and frogs his lover sneaked into his cell, he was just able to make it through. By the time he got out, he was skeletal, his five-foot-ten-inch frame weighing less than 90 pounds. He couldn't stand on his own and had to be carried out on a stretcher. The young woman not only helped him recover, she also did the inconceivable, feeding and caring for her baby while she continued to work; and the child actually made it. I later learned that in 1989, the couple was let out of the camp and got married. Most of Yodok's love stories were neither as pleasant nor as long; prolonged malnutrition tends to refocus one's desires.

Yet love endured, in spite of everything. It even had its heroes, like the thirty-year-old fellow who arrived at the camp in 1986. He was a good-looking man, and well built, too. According to the numbers floating around camp, he had been intimate with at least twenty-eight different women. His success came in spite of, or maybe because of, his reputation as a Don Juan. His pleasure did come at a price, however, for his conquests cost him three trips to the sweatbox, each lasting three months. No prisoner had ever survived so many repeated stints, but he got out safe and sound every time, on his feet and able to walk without help, as though nothing much had happened. We called him the man of steel. His hardiness and sexual prowess made him one of Yodok's most celebrated and honored prisoners. Even the security agents were impressed and treated him with a certain deference.

I don't know whether he is still alive, but if he is, I am sure he can be found in camp number 15, because every tour in the sweatbox added five extra years to his prison sentence.

열다섯

FIFTEEN

SOJOURN IN
THE MOUNTAIN

My last two years in the camp were not as trying as the previous eight had been. From 1985 to 1987, I was lucky enough to be transferred to a less difficult detail in a remote part of the camp, where I was able to find relative solitude and extricate myself from the familiar routine of paradox and cruelty. The paradox was in the nonchalance of the guards, in their lack of interest, ultimately, in how we were performing our work, and in the cynical black humor we ourselves deployed as a defense against our dreadful existence. The cruelty was in the punishments and accidents. Yet there were also adventures, enjoyable ones even, which I still recall with a certain fondness.

One day in May, while a couple dozen youngsters and I were up in the mountains gathering wild ginseng for a campaign to "support the Great Leader by earning dollars for the Party," we suddenly found ourselves nose to nose with a bear. A friend of mine who had gone off to urinate had seen a moving black mass and, to convince himself that it was nothing, threw a rock at it. The bear roared with anger and started chasing us. Never had I imagined that such a big animal could run so fast! Fortunately he lost interest fairly quickly. We ran a bit farther, then stopped in the middle of a field. We stood catching our breath when we suddenly realized that wild ginseng was growing all around us. The bear had served as our guide!

Thanks to the kindness of certain guards, I also had the good fortune of being selected, along with two other prisoners, to be a shepherd. This task was more difficult than one might suppose because we were responsible for several hundred sheep, whose number was continually being verified. Yet the job provided relative freedom, along with a steady supply of sheep's milk, a handsome supplement to my ordinary diet. When my traps worked, I was also able to catch an occasional rodent or snake. Then from April to August 1986, I was given the even better position of assistant beekeeper, which allowed me to benefit from the confidence of the guards, who harvested honey behind their superiors' backs.

Having come to know the mountain well, the guards often ordered me to assist with burials. The one I remember most was that of Kim Su-ra, a young girl who died on February 16, 1986, the anniversary of Kim Jong-il's birthday. She was the only girl in a family of five children, and she was very beautiful. The poor girl had been suffering from tuberculosis and malnutrition for a long time. In preparation for the ceremony honoring our Dear Leader's birthday, she got dressed up with all the care and energy she could muster. The annual event was often an occasion for announcing a prisoner release, and she hoped her family might be among the chosen. But she collapsed upon arriving at the ceremony and never got up again. Since we all loved her very much and thought she deserved to be honored, we pieced together a coffin out of discarded planks from the neighboring sawmill. As we carried her coffin up the mountain on our shoulders, her body could nevertheless be seen through the holes in the wood. When we got to the burial spot, the ground was frozen to a depth of almost two feet, and we had to build a fire to soften the earth before we could start digging. The following spring, the ground shifted slightly, and the corpse started coming up. I re-covered it so that the girl might still have a decent resting place.

Alone in the heights, I escaped the abuse of guards: the blows, the forced labor, the sweatbox. Beatings didn't appear on the official list of sanctioned punishments, but they were the camp's most common currency. No trifle was too small to serve as a pretext for a beating—of a child or an adult. For example, the South Korean government used balloons to drop leaflets on their northern neighbor. Upon finding such a leaflet, a prisoner was supposed to turn it over to a guard or tear it up right away without reading it. The problem was, despite the paper's weight and roughness, it was much prized for its potential hygienic use. One day, a newly arrived and still unsuspecting prisoner happened upon one such crumpled sheet and rushed to hand it over to a guard. The agent looked very smug at first, but as he began to unfold the sheet, his expression suddenly changed. The paper had already been used. The guard beat the hapless prisoner with such furor that he was unable to move for several days.

I somehow was always able to dodge such thrashings and avoid the camp's most dangerous work details. Not all children were so fortunate. In the spring of 1986, three of my schoolmates were transferred to the gold mine, where their job was setting and detonating dynamite. They had to light the fuse first and run for cover second. They must have been especially tired one day, because they didn't manage to get very far before the blast went off. Two of them were killed. The third, who was partially protected by a turn in the tunnel, had half his face blown off. Poor kids! The guards had no scruples about how they used them. They actually preferred children for the job, because they were smaller and quicker. Gold mine accidents were second only to malnutrition as Yodok's leading cause of mortality. They were responsible for more deaths than even the felling of trees, not to mention the innumerable casualties that resulted from cave-ins and mishandled tools.

Soft-skinned city boy that I was, I was lucky to get out of there alive. Yet the harsh living conditions and never-ending work were precisely what saved me, because they left me no time to dwell on my condition. My every minute was accounted for. There were lessons to follow under threats from brutalizing instructors, trees to chop down, sacks of gold-laden earth to haul, rabbits to watch, fields of corn to harvest. My life was absorbed entirely in my efforts to get by and obey orders. I was, fortunately, able to accept my condition as fated. A clear-eyed view of the hell I had landed in certainly would have thrown me deeper into despair. There is nothing like thought to deepen one's gloom.

Yet I wasn't always able to repel the feeling of misfortune. I had dreams in which I died or witnessed the death of another prisoner, crushed by falling trees, for example, or stoned, like the unlucky hanged fugitives. At night, all the scenes I tried to erase from my memory returned: the cries of pain, the disfigured faces, the crushed limbs. When my eyes closed, the doors that shut out my fears and memories opened wide. Occasionally I saw Pyongyang again, something that caused me strange and useless pain; at times I wondered whether the camp was the dream, or Pyongyang. I was a bit like Zhuangzi (Chuang Tzu), who wakes up asking himself, Where does reality start? Where does the dream end? Was it I who dreamed of being a butterfly, or the butterfly who dreamed of being me? My obsession with death was not confined to nightmares, but sometimes appeared in daytime, disturbing my fanatical desire to survive. Death often seemed preferable to the hell all around me; but the thought of the cold wet earth that would swallow me was enough to turn me back toward life.

As the years passed, another feeling began to disturb my daily existence: the feeling of injustice, which grew sharper when I considered the discrepancy between everything I had been taught and all that I was living. My opinions evolved much as had my grandmother's—surprise gave way to a sense of injustice, which in turn transformed into indignation and silent denunciation. We had always been taught to think and speak in accordance with our Great Leader's irrecusable axioms, but the guards' actions continually contradicted them. I had memorized almost entirely *A Letter to New Korea's Much Beloved Children*, which Kim Il-sung wrote for the occasion of the Day of Children, "who are the treasure of our country and its future. . . ."* And yet I was being made to pay for my grandfather's crimes. I was no longer the jewel in Kim Il-sung's eye. I was a prisoner: filthy, tattered, hungry, spent. All those beautiful words had been flouted with perfect impunity.

Why had we been cut off from the world? Why had we been labeled "redeemable" if we weren't to be given the means of reintegrating into the life of the country—especially since every bit of news in North Korea was filtered through state propaganda any-

---

*The letter dates from May 5, 1946. See Kim Il-sung, *Complete Works*, vol. 2 (Pyongyang: 1980), 193, foreign language edition.

way? All attempts to communicate with the outside were severely punished. One prisoner who had wealthy family members living in Japan managed to get in touch with them by bribing a guard; when camp authorities found out, the guard became a prisoner. Even our own release—which we had been awaiting for years—was only announced to us at the last possible moment.

열여섯

TEN YEARS IN
THE CAMP: THANK YOU,
KIM IL-SUNG!

And then one day the nightmare was over. We'd lately sensed a change in the guards' attitude toward us, but we hadn't really thought much of it. It was barely noticeable, and there was no way to know what it meant. Some of the guards, most notably the one who had gotten my uncle out of hard labor, let us understand that it was in our best interest to keep a low profile and redouble our efforts. But such suggestions were not uncommon. The authorities often damaged false hopes in front of us to inspire harder work.

On February 16, 1987, all the prisoners in the village were summoned to the large meeting hall for the chance to celebrate the birth and sing the praises of Kim Jong-il. The camp's security chief, wearing his full dress uniform, gave a speech about the benevolence of our Dear Leader. At the end of the address, the prisoners were directed through a choral rendition of the famous "Song of General Kim Il-sung":

Along the Changback mountain
Lies a trail of blood
Along the river Amnok
Lies a trail of blood
Still today, above the flower bouquet of free Korea
Shines forth that glorious trail
Oh! Oh! Our general
The general Kim Il-sung

The security chief then announced that some of us were to be released. As the official got set to read the list of selected prisoners, a shiver ran through the crowd, followed by complete silence. February 16 was the usual date for these announcements, but this time there would be a surprise: I heard my family's name being called! On the instant, it was difficult to understand what that really meant. My uncle, sitting next to me, was overwrought and struggled not to let his happiness show. It was inappropriate to feel joy at leaving a place that so effectively righted one's mistaken ideologies and that was so immersed in the thought of Kim Il-sung! The other names were called out without our taking notice. My uncle leaned over and whispered in my ear, "We might still get out of this! We might still get out of this!"

I didn't know what to think. The news was both extraordinary and terribly disturbing. I would have liked to discuss it with my grandmother and father, but they were sick that day and had been unable to attend the ceremony. The head of the camp then explained that President Kim Il-sung and his son, our dear leader Kim Jong-il, had decided that, given the ideological progress demonstrated by the aforementioned prisoners, an opportunity would be given them to work for the fatherland outside the confines of Yodok. The remaining prisoners should let this gesture stand as proof of our leaders' boundless solicitude.

Following these brief comments, two prisoner representatives stepped forward to address the crowd. The first was a prisoner scheduled for release, the second would be staying on. So that they might prepare for their speeches, the two men had been made privy, under the greatest secrecy, to the list of departing prisoners. The representative who was leaving Yodok was the first to speak. Concealing any hint of hatred he might still have harbored for the Party, he extolled the wisdom of our leaders, their forethought, and, above all, the Party's magnanimity: "Due to the grace of our Great Leader, the comrade Kim Il-sung, we will be set free in spite of our former crimes. We thank the Party from the bottom of our hearts and will do all in our power to be worthy of its decision. A debt of gratitude is also owed the directors of the Yodok camp, who helped us realize the seriousness of our misdeeds, reeducated us and our families, fed and cared for us, in the purest spirit of patriotism and revolution. . . ."

The representative of the remaining prisoners spoke next. Having already spent ten years in Yodok, he too had hoped to be among the departing prisoners; but it was not to be, and no one would ever give a reason why. He was, nevertheless, expected to prepare a speech thanking the Party and its Great Leader for their providential decision to keep behind the prisoners not yet ready to rejoin the revolutionary struggle as ordinary members of Korean life. "The Party is giving us the chance to continue bettering ourselves. On behalf of everyone staying here, I want to offer our thanks and to promise that we will work even harder from now on, so that we may one day merit our release." The ceremony ended with everyone wishing for the good health and longevity of our Great Leader. My uncle and I rushed back to the hut. Our two patients couldn't believe their ears. I think my grandmother shed a few tears—or perhaps it was my father. Mi-ho remained silent, but her face was glowing.

The next day, the liberated families were summoned to the security office of the village, where we each had to sign a document promising never to reveal any information about Yodok or about what they had seen during their incarceration. We acknowledged that sharing a single word on this subject justified "appropriate punishment"—a return trip to Yodok, for example, or to a worse place. We signed the documents with a fingerprint and waited to see what would happen next. There were only about ten families in all, a number so small that, in sum, it caused more tears and bitterness than joy in Yodok. So many had arrived at the camp when we had—or even before—but were not set free. Were they to die in that cursed place? Every time our eyes met, I felt a vague sense of guilt. I tried to avoid them and to escape that look of hopelessness, sometimes tinged with hate. Among the remaining prisoners was a girl who was a little older than I. I had worked with her a few times, and we were friends. When she heard I was leaving, she couldn't stop crying—owing as much to her fate as our impending separation. I couldn't find the words to console her. What could I say? What did she have to hope for, when the only reason for hope was postponed indefinitely? I was also terribly sad to be leaving Yi Sae-bong and his stories of Japanese life. There were other prisoners who had offered me their friendship and help during very hard times. With them I had shared rat meat and heaped maledictions on the Wild Boar; with them I had buried the beautiful young girl and taken revenge on the corpse of the snitch. I had burst out laughing when a prisoner farted at an edifying moment of a revolutionary film, and had shivered in the mountains under the falling rain. The memo-ries of everything that had happened in the past decade were sweeping over me. I think I was actually afraid of leaving that place, of no longer seeing those mountain ridges all around me. Deep down, I had come to love them. They had been the bars of my prison and the framework of my life. They were my suffering and my being, bound indissolubly together. My most poignant memories were attached to the place where I had suffered the most. It was a strange, complicated feeling, for Yodok was still a hellish, inhuman place.

Though I was happy about being released, the prospect of leaving the place that had been my universe for so long filled me with anxiety. Ten years. It was a big chunk of life! What would be waiting for me when I got out? Besides joy, I also felt a certain moroseness. I had seen the same complexity of feeling among earlier departing prisoners, naively believing that I would be different—happy—that the joy would be written all over my face and overwhelm every other emotion. Now that my liberation had arrived, my thoughts and emotions were as confused as theirs had been. I had grown up nourishing myself on rats and frogs; I thought of this as my life, and it was. I had grown accustomed to it; changing worlds, from one moment to the next, was strange to me. For the adults it was different, because they had other references in their lives, but they weren't aglow with joy, either. Grandmother, for one, was not at all expansive. "Ah, well, I guess I won't die in this camp after all," she declared flatly. "So in the end I will get to see my other children." What I didn't understand at the time was how angry she felt—along with my father and uncle—about the ten years she had lost at Yodok, about the impossibility of ever rediscovering a satisfactory life.

These reactions were on the affective order: I was going to miss the places, the people, the friendships, the shared moments. But the day-to-day struggle for life at camp number 15 was no cause for nostalgic sentimentality. It had taught me very little over the years.

Some veterans of the Soviet gulags speak of the camps as having been their university, but it wasn't so for me. The only lesson I got pounded into me was about man's limitless capacity for vice—that and the fact that social distinctions vanish in a concentration camp. I once believed that man was different from other animals, but Yodok showed me that reality doesn't support this opinion. In the camp, there was no difference between man and beast, except maybe that a very hungry human was capable of stealing food from its little ones while an animal, perhaps, was not. I also saw many people die in the camp, and their deaths looked like that of other animals.

Before leaving, we gave our tools as parting gifts to the friends and neighbors who were staying behind. These rusted, twisted things were among the only belongings we were allowed to treat as our own.

Liberation day finally arrived. It was toward the very end of February 1987. Several prisoners accompanied us as far as they could, waving good-bye. It was a very sad scene. We knew we would likely never see them again, but we tried to be reassuring, to affirm that their day would also come and that they should take good care. They nodded in agreement, without showing how slim they thought these hopes and how ludicrous this advice. We left in the same kind of truck that had brought us to the camp ten years earlier. When it started up, I was taken back to our departure from Pyongyang, and to my mother's tear-lined face as it receded into the distance. The vision struck me with new and unexpected force—for I had all but forgotten my mother. Her memory had become so faded and distant it hardly seemed real. Now, as the truck slowly spat and rattled into motion, her image raced back to me in a flash. In an instant I understood that leaving the camp had finally made a reunion pos-

sible and that from now on I could start thinking of her again without it being simply painful and absurd. I was bowled over by the
intrusion of this memory and the meaning it might have.

We drove for about twenty-five miles before arriving at a village
that would be our temporary home until more permanent lodgings
could be found for us. In North Korea, each county (*do*) is divided
into several cantons (*gun*), and each canton into several districts.
For the time being, we were not permitted to leave our *gun*, which
was a part of the county of Yodok. This restriction was applied to all
recently released prisoners. We spent our first night in a run-down
little hotel where I dreamt I was still in the camp. When I woke up,
I still thought I was there. But a glance at the white floors brusquely
reminded me that I was "out." In the camp, a bell woke us up every
morning at five. Here, there was no bell. I was overtaken by a very
odd feeling, and it took time to fully grasp that I had entered a different universe. The countryside stretched out in every direction.
We were at first assigned to an agricultural part of the *gun*, and for
a time we lived and worked on a collective farm. Now that we were
free citizens, our diet was much better and usually consisted of rice,
soybean curd, and whiting. This was in 1987, before the famine had
taken root and spread throughout the country.

We were only at the farm a short while when my uncle managed
to receive authorization to move to Pyungsung, where his valuable
skills as a biochemist could be put to better use. The rest of us had
our assignment to Yodok confirmed, and that's where we stayed
until April.

Every district in North Korea is administered by two committees:
one administrative, and the other political. Upon reentering civilian
life, the Security Force handed us over to a Work Section controlled
by the former, which assigned us to agricultural work on a collec-

tive farm. We were, of course, marked as former prisoners—in North Korea, identification cards always give a citizen's most recent occupation. Mine indicated that I had worked for army unit 2915. That wouldn't mean much to a civilian, but a security agent could immediately understand he was dealing with a former political prisoner. We were constantly being watched, in our neighborhood and at our work, both by security agents and ubiquitous snitches, who were just as plentiful on the outside as they had been in the camp. Everyone in North Korea, of course, is under surveillance; as former prisoners, ours was just a little tighter. The odd thing was they had no reason to watch me; I had a policeman inside my head. The camp had trained me so well that I was still greeting every agent I came across with a sweeping, ninety-degree bow. This made all my new friends laugh, which gradually helped me break the habit.

My family and I had no desire to stay in the countryside, but citizens who wanted to leave their *gun* had to obtain permission from the director of their work group, the police, and the local security office. Former prisoners also required a supplementary authorization from the State Security Agency. Fortunately, many of our relatives had avoided the camps, and several of them—most notably, two of my dad's sisters and my first uncle—were ready to help us. Because they were related to political prisoners, they had long ago been dispersed to small towns and villages at a remove from the capital. (One of my aunts thus wound up in Changjin, a mountain village made famous by the dramatic defeat dealt there to the Americans during MacArthur's retreat in December 1950.)

Yet my relatives had remained free—as free as anyone can be in North Korea—and by giving the bureaucratic wheels a generous greasing, my first uncle was eventually able to reassemble my father's side of the family in Musan. There he eventually met one of our former Yodok neighbors, who told him of our release. He quickly arranged for the whole family to take the long, difficult train ride to our *kun*. The reunion was very moving. At first, my uncles didn't recognize my sister and me, but after a moment of silence, we threw ourselves into one another's arms. They hadn't had word of us in all that time and had feared the worst. I remember there were outbursts of laughter and crying all through the night.

Prior to our relatives' visit, we had been wearing the clothes the security agents had given us upon leaving the camp. The departing prisoners were all given the same clothes. While slightly more presentable than the camp uniforms, they all shared the same cut, which lacked every hint of elegance and made us look every bit like former prisoners. Thanks to our relatives, who came bearing gifts of Japanese clothes and underwear, we were instantly transformed from paupers into rich people. My uncle and my two aunts stayed with us for almost a week and did everything in their power to brighten our spirits. And boy, did we ever need it!

The peasants with whom we worked had little sympathy for our plight. As far as they were concerned, former counterrevolutionary prisoners were by definition bad, shady people. They knew about Yodok, of course, just as every North Korean knows about the country's network of camps. What people don't know is the number of camps there are, how many people they hold, or what happens to people when they get there. But most North Koreans share an exceptional innocence and honesty; in time, these peasants realized our incarceration didn't necessarily mean we were bad people. As the distance between us lessened, gradually we were able to share parts of our story with them, though the details remained vague, for the sake of everyone's safety. By the end, I think they actually came to like us and feel genuine compassion for our fate.

Days on the collective farm began with a general assembly, which provided us with our daily ration of political manna. The Party secretary who ran the meetings was usually content to rehash one of Kim Il-sung's recent addresses or to read an editorial from *Rodong Sinmun*, but when excited about some recent event, he could drone on for as long as an hour and a half. A Party cadre then took roll call before sending us off to get our work assignment from the office of management. During wintertime, most agricultural workers were shifted to indoor maintenance work. North Korean peasants don't know the meaning of vacation. They work so hard for their measly compensation, which sometimes isn't even paid out in real money but rather in ration tickets. Until 1990, these tickets could be redeemed practically anywhere, but they have since lost all value in many parts of the country.

Thanks to my uncle and to the countless gifts he distributed, my family was soon moved to a small town near the district's industrial center. We lived there from 1987 to 1990, exchanging exhausting agricultural work for less taxing jobs in shops and factories. Leaving the farm also saved us from being classified as peasants, a caste to which my family otherwise would have been condemned forever. In North Korea, the children of peasants are destined to remain peasants. They are systematically prevented from climbing the social ladder and can only advance by joining the army or by greasing a lot of palms—an option that presupposes having connections abroad. In the past, peasants could also pull themselves out of the underclass by marrying a city dweller, but the laws were changed in 1988. A marriage between a peasant and a city dweller now means social regression for the latter, who has no choice but to move to the country.

열일곱

SEVENTEEN

THE NORTH KOREAN
PARADISE

Our release from the camp did little to improve my father's health. He had been sick for a long time, having let an ulcer condition go untreated when we were still in Pyongyang. Once in Yodok, an operation was out of the question. Truth be told, given the state of hospitals in North Korea, I'm not sure he would have come out of it alive anyway. The good side, if it can be put that way, was that at Yodok his poor health and fragile constitution saved him from being assigned to hard-labor details. He also was fortunate to have good hands and was a competent addition to the woodworking shop. My father was a calm, taciturn man who resigned to fate without protest. Like Mi-ho, his greatest asset in life was probably his ability to draw no attention to himself. In all our time in Yodok, he was never once approached to work as a snitch. The ten years he spent in the camp were lost years, no question about it—full of hardship and longing for his wife—but they were also strangely peaceful. Yet his lot had been too much to endure. His extinguished artistic dreams, the absence of his wife, the years spent making stools and broomsticks: it was all so much pain and suffering—and for what?

His illness worsened at the end of November 1987. The pain was not as acute as it had been on several earlier occasions, but he was now bedridden. I remember his last day. He was lying calmly in bed with his eyes closed, when his whole body suddenly went slack. He made a little gesture with his hand, smiling slightly—what I later realized was his final farewell. That's how he died, without our even realizing it. That scene changed my perception of death. Previously, it always wore a mask of terror; I never imagined it could be so peaceful. Since then, death no longer scares me. My father showed me it could be a moment for smiling.

For the next two days, we sat watch over my father's body, in accordance with Korean tradition. Family and friends gathered to drink, eat noodles and play cards; neighbors dropped by to help with all the preparations; and the North Korean state gave us an allotment for thirty liters of alcohol, as was its wont on the occasion of a citizen's death. With the aid of some bribery, the thirty liters became a hundred liters, a volume approaching what was needed for a proper funeral. I buried my father up in the mountains, in a spot with a beautiful view. Koreans believe that a well-chosen burial site brings prosperity to the descendants of the deceased. I sometimes think this might account for all the good luck I have had since.

My father died without ever seeing my mother again. It didn't have to be that way. Though our movement was restricted, she was free to apply for a travel permit to come visit us. The real obstacle was that we didn't know were she was. In the West, such information can be had by consulting a phone book, checking with the police, or placing an advertisement in a newspaper. In North Korea, these options aren't available. Ultimately, it was luck that brought us together. My mother's youngest sister, who lived in Nampo, met an ex-prisoner from Yodok who kept in touch with a number of his old campmates, some of whom knew our whereabouts. Through them, we got our aunt's address. But this stroke of luck only made me realize how unready I was for a reunion. While I wanted very much to see my mother, I still had lingering doubts—kept alive largely by my grandmother—about the circumstances under which she had gotten the divorce. My father, influenced perhaps by his mother's unflattering insinuations, hadn't made any inquiries among former acquaintances who might put him in touch with his wife. Were there other reasons why I hesitated to see my mother? For the last ten years, Grandmother had raised us, supported us, protected us. We had become her children. Did I suspect she feared that a reunion with our mother would cause her to lose us? Whatever the reason, I didn't use the address until after my grandmother's death in 1989.

Two years after our release, Grandmother was still in good health. She stayed at home mostly, sometimes doing light fieldwork, such as weeding and gathering food for the rabbits. The start of the summer of 1989 was extremely hot. One day—June 25, to be exact—Grandmother and I had a stupid argument about what she had made me for lunch. Later regretting the way I had acted, I resolved to come home early to offer my apologies, but when I arrived, I found the house empty. Then the neighbors came running over to tell me Grandmother had fallen in the middle of a field. I ran as fast as I could only to find her lying there motionless. We carried her back to the house, but alas, she had stopped breathing. She had mostly likely died of a cerebral hemorrhage. It was a terrible blow to my sister and me. We had been so close. She was the link that kept the family pieces connected. Mi-ho and I were now alone. Later on, I missed her with less desperation. She had guarded much of her beauty until the age of sixty, but after one year in the camp, she was white-haired, wrinkled, and toothless. Her illnesses, too—the pellagra and an internal hemorrhage—had left their mark. But, proud daughter of Cheju, she had surmounted every test.

A few weeks after Grandmother's death, my sister and I wrote to Nampo for information about our mother, and in January 1990, we got permission to travel to Pyongyang, where we learned she was living. She tearfully recounted the events of the thirteen miserable years since our departure. Then it was our turn to tell what had become of us, while she sat there staring, mouth agape. She didn't interrupt us once, but neither did she venture a single word against the regime. Had her loyalty survived intact? All she could bring herself to say was, "You were so unlucky. That's fate. . . ." In the wake of our deportation to Yodok, she waited for her turn to come. She was sure she would soon be interrogated and sent to join us. But the security agents never showed up, and so, eventually, she went to them. She wanted permission to join us, but the agents knew how to discourage her. "Do you really want to be condemned?" they asked. "You know, we might also send away all your brothers and sisters and all their children."

My mother thought she would never see us again. Instead of offering her a little hope, the agents assured her we would be staying at Yodok until our dying days. There was nothing else for her to do. She went home and unpacked all the food and clothing she planned to take on her trip. For a long time afterward, she lived alone, depressed and sick.

The little apartment she now occupied in central Pyongyang had one main room, a kitchen, and a little laundry room. Whenever we came to visit her, she would spend hours cooking us wonderful meals, delighted at the resumption of her motherly duties. For a time she considered leaving her apartment and moving closer to us, but I dissuaded her. She was so lucky to be living in Pyongyang and to be working for the People's Office of Services, the government department responsible for the distribution of consumable goods. I promised we would come visit as often as we could. During my sojourn in Yodok, I had been angry at her for not joining us. I hadn't understood her situation. I didn't know that having already separated my parents, the state could also force them to divorce. I hope my mother isn't angry with me now for having left the country, and I hope she understands me better than I understood her.

Life followed its course. A few months after grandmother's death, my sister and I moved to Pyungsung to live with my uncle, who got married shortly after. Mi-ho decided to enter nursing school. Now that we were out of the camp, I had a chance to get to know her again. At Yodok, our work duties had always kept us apart. While I was generally working outdoors, she spent all of her time at the camp's textile factory, only coming home for quick snatches of food and sleep. Only now that we were out did I realize how much she had changed. She was eighteen years old, and astoundingly beautiful. Back at the camp, the uniforms, the filth, and the prolonged malnutrition ensured that no one looked attractive. Once free, though, Mi-ho's beauty became impossible to overlook, and I was proud when smitten friends complimented me on her physical charm. She had many suitors—too many even for my taste. An officer of the Korean People's Army was especially persistent. He seemed like a nice guy and he was remarkably strong physically. He once won a prize in a national competition in the Korean martial art of tae kwon do. To curry my favor, he often brought me rice and heating fuel that he stole from his barracks, which made me a bit weary. Looking back now, he actually was a rather odd character. As chauffeur to a division general, he systematically tried to run over dogs he saw on the street. The hobby proved to be his undoing. One day he skidded out of control while chasing a particularly fleet-footed dog and drove the general's car into a rice paddy. He got sentenced to a year in jail, and I never saw him again.

Truth be told, I enjoyed his conversation and missed him when he was gone. When I left Yodok, I also left all my friends. I later reestablished contact with several of them on the outside, but these relations were always rocky. That's how it was with one of my former Yodok teammates, who survived outside the camp on money sent by his sister from Japan. He was a rich man by North Korean standards, and his wealth gave him enormous power. Among other things, it enabled him to divorce the wife his father had arranged for him. Give a bureaucrat a "little gift" and he'll miraculously turn up all those files that have been lying in abeyance for months. My friend later used the same method to smooth over the legal questions that emerged from his beating his second wife, the fight he had with her new lover, and his second request for divorce. A little grease kept everything nice and quiet. That's the way things usually work in North Korea: money and violence stand in for law and order. We even have a saying for it: "The law is far; the fist is close." The regime that never tires of denouncing capitalism has birthed a society where money is king—more so than any capitalist society I have visited. This was the saving grace for Koreans who made the mistake of moving back from Japan. Money was their only defense against the mistrust of their fellow

Koreans and the outright hostility of the police, who always suspected them of espionage and disturbing the public peace.

As for violence, it was everywhere. Anything that vaguely
recalled affection or compassion was banished from the realm.
Everyone threatened and was threatened, beat and was beaten.
After the education I received at Yodok, I too became violent and
had no qualms about hurting people. It wasn't until I left North
Korea that I started acting more like a human being again. I
remember once being attacked, on April 15, Kim Il-sung's birthday.
As on every vacation day, most people just moped around the city,
drinking and looking for a brawl. Fighting is always against the law
in North Korea, but fighting on a holiday as solemn as Kim Il-
sung's birthday is considered a political crime, punishable by hard
labor. I was strolling with a group of friends—my gang, if you
will—when we crossed paths with another gang. A few insults
later, a fight broke out. At one point I was pinned down by several
men and started swinging like a madman. Somehow, one of my
punches landed in the eye of a former marine rifleman, who was
the head of the gang. He reeled back in pain. I took advantage of
his hesitation and ran away as fast as I could. It was a good thing,
too; a little later, some agents from the Security Force came and
arrested several people. That evening, I was sitting outside chatting
with my sister's boyfriend when I saw the rival gang coming up the
street. There were around twenty of them, a few wielding axes and
shovels. This time I was really scared. But my sister's suitor
stepped forward: "If you want to attack Kang Chol-hwan, you'll
have to kill me first!" Thanks to his introduction, I was able to start
a conversation with the gang leader whom I had punched. I offered
my apologies, and he presented his compliments: "You are strong,
Kang Chol-hwan. That's the first time anyone has punched me like
that." We became friends, and from then on I was his protégé. The

hierarchy of the street remained intact and I had nothing more to fear.

My behavior changed only gradually. In the camp I was beaten without being able to hit back, but now that I was out, I fought back systematically. Yet violence was repulsive to me. I fought and was mad at myself for fighting. But no matter how much I tried to avoid it, it always lay in my path. One day a gang started beating me with bottles, and instead of trying to fight back, I ran to find a nearby policeman whom I'd previously plied with little gifts. He tracked down my attackers and locked them up. Then he called me in. "Go into their cell and beat the crap out of them if you want," he offered. "Only I don't want any trouble, so you can't kill them." I started punching one of them, but then felt so ashamed I stopped and left the cell.

After that, I signed up for a tae kwon do course to help me control my emotions and stop people from messing with me. Once word got around, I was left in peace. One of the interesting things about North Korean hoodlums is the contempt they have for former political prisoners. Many gang members spend time in prison— that's a right everyone has—and though their families aren't dragged down with them, they consider the plight of Yodok's political prisoners a cakewalk compared to what they go through. The horrors these ruffians face in prison is on another level altogether. As far as they are concerned, "the little morons from camp number 15" have it good.

I eventually got a job as a deliveryman for my *gun*'s Office of Distribution. Since the region where I worked was very mountainous and there weren't enough trucks to go around, we usually did our routes using oxcarts. (Making a virtue of necessity, Kim Il-sung once wrote an homage to this mode of transport.) I enjoyed the work; we were always showing up with long-awaited supplies, so the people we met were happy to see us, greeting us with open arms and sometimes giving us tips. More important, by taking advantage of the price disparities between Pyongyang and the provinces, we were able to do a little side business. A pair of shoes that cost 5 to 10 North Korean won when it left the factory in Pyongyang could be sold for eight to ten times that in the provinces—almost half a typical factory worker's monthly salary.

In the beginning, I took my work very seriously, tackling it with all the energy and efficiency I could muster. My years in Yodok had trained me well! My colleagues and superiors appreciated my work, and I was tight with my local Party secretary whom I'd once supplied with hard-to-find wood. To show his gratitude, he regularly assigned me the easiest routes, which left me plenty of time to rest. As was inevitable, I gradually lost my enthusiasm for the work. Without the guards at my back I saw no particular reason to exert myself any more than my colleagues. What I wanted was to visit other regions of the county and to see if there was any business to be made. So, after paying off the Party secretary and receiving my traveling papers, I started travelling around to other *guns* to purchase merchandise, which I then transported by truck or through private individuals. I bought wild ginseng, traded alcohol for shoes, sold bear bile and civet cat navels—which apparently work wonders on victims of stroke. I wasn't making a fortune, but business was good. Before long I was ready to abandon the dung wagons and oxcarts and focus on developing my commercial ventures, which I did with the support of my friendly Party secretary.

The People's Office of Services had two functions: to organize the distribution of goods to nonactive parts of the population, and to offset inefficiencies in the rationing system by procuring and distributing goods the system couldn't supply. These included everything from hair products to pastries, shoes to clothing, bread to bicycles. As the Party's main distribution network slipped into ever-deepening paralysis, the supplementary network became indispensable, though clunky and untenable. If we needed leather or gasoline, for example, we had to go to the army, where the person who ran the gas tank wielded more power than his commander-in-chief! I once procured a year's supply of gasoline for the price of a Seiko watch. The parallel distribution network was by far the more active part of the system, and it offered an entrepreneur the chance to make a lot of money. On my own relatively modest level, that's exactly what I did. I pocketed about 1,000 won per month, enough to pass for rich in North Korea. For most of the population, though, the situation was going from bad to worse. Eventually even ration tickets, the most basic currency, stopped being honored, because nothing was showing up at the stores, neither food, nor clothes, nor cleaning products.

The collapse happened suddenly. The clearest measure was the whiting that Koreans traditionally hang out to dry on the walls of their houses: the visible decline in the fish's numbers, which began in 1988, was a sign writ large of the nation's economic crisis. By 1990, drying fish were nowhere to be seen. That was also the year when the country's rice distribution was severely mismanaged. Here is one aspect of the current famine that doesn't attract enough attention. Besides the production problems that arise from inadequate work incentives, fertilizers, and working tractors, there is also the problem of distribution. The Yodok canton, for example, was still running surpluses as late as 1990, but no trains were available for transport. The only alternative transportation was the country's aging fleet of run-down trucks, which kept breaking down on the unpaved roads. Rice that was needed in the city sat rotting in the countryside, while manufactured goods the country people needed never left the city.

As the situation worsened, peasants began raising their own goats and dogs and expending less energy on the collective farms. Considering how little their monthly salary of 100 to 150 won bought, they had little choice. A dog cost 300 won, a goat 400, a jar of honey 150. To keep from starving, peasants began cultivating thousands of hills abandoned by the collective farms, turning much of the countryside into a Far West of appropriated tracts. Demonstrating the same courage and tenacity I later discovered among the merchants of Namdaemun,* these peasants often worked their new plots at night after putting in a full day on the collective farms. Under the direction of incompetent, corrupt bureaucrats, they spent the daylight hours dozing off and dragging their feet. But at night, when time came to provide for their families, they worked like demons. Unfortunately, private farming was a major cause of flooding in 1996–97, because deforested slopes susceptible to soil erosion led to landslides and a dangerous buildup of the riverbeds. Though the Party was fervently opposed to private land use, the peasant movement grew so strong that the Party had no choice but to give ground. It never formally changed its laws, but it grudgingly tolerates the practice, and is content merely to remind the peasants that in the Democratic People's Republic of Korea no land belongs to a single owner, and that anyone taking possession of a plot risks having it confiscated. The movement and its revolts have been so vast that the Party has only moved to dismantle the most egregious land grabs. This is all very revealing of North Korea's present situation and its inevitable slide from communism to capitalism.

---

*Namdaemun is a large market in Seoul that is active day and night.

This wild trend toward privatization—or appropriation, if you prefer—explains why peasants are now having an easier time procuring food than workers who live in small towns, where famine has struck hardest. But the peasants suffer from another privation, of clothes, which they must buy from outlaw traveling salesmen. These merchants buy their stock on the cities' black markets or from one of the handful of surviving sweatshops and factories. Sometimes clothes are smuggled in from China. When I was still living in North Korea in the early 1990s, the terms of exchange were heavily weighed against the peasants. A pair of 40-won nylon socks cost them two kilos of corn. An egg earned them 1 won; a bottle of oil, 10 to 15 won; a chicken, 60 won; but it cost 100 to 150 won to buy fabric for a suit of clothes; 400 won for a pair of Japanese-sewn pants; 100 to 130 won for a short-sleeved shirt made in China—and 250 if it were made in Japan. This explains why relatives of former Japanese residents always came to visit North Korea with armloads of socks, clothes, and alcohol, whose exchange value was astronomical.

The generosity of our family in Japan certainly made a big difference in our lives. It enabled us to purchase the benevolence of guards and minders and slowly to inch our way closer to Pyongyang. As a matter of law, former prisoners are not allowed to leave the zone where they have been assigned to live. As a matter of practice, bribery makes everything possible. We wrote to relatives asking for help, careful to disguise our meaning, so as not to provoke the censors. North Koreans are permitted to send letters out of the country as long as they don't criticize or complain about the regime. When our relatives suddenly received a letter from us after ten years of silence, they had a fairly good notion of what had become of us. During the years of our disappearance, they had made several attempts to visit us in North Korea and were repeatedly turned away by the police, who told them we were on vacation. There was much concern in Japan about all the North Koreans who had suddenly left on extended vacations. Petitions got circulated about the issue. Korean residents in Japan appeared on television to talk about the disappearance of their relatives. Maybe some of this even played a role in our release, though my grandfather's death probably had more to do with that. While we will probably never discover what really became of him, it was believed that the authorities waited for a convicted political criminal to die before releasing his family.

Thanks to the power of money, we escaped the dreadful life of the North Korean backwater. Want to make a telephone call? You'll have to pass through the operator . . . and hold the line. . . . And to reach Japan, endless troubles. Officially, of course, it is quite possible. In fact, only special—that is, tapped—telephone centers are equipped for the job, and they only accept foreign currency. Want to go out? There is only one movie theater for the whole canton. And while the prices are risibly cheap, the film will infallibly be some glorification of North Korea, its army, the anti-Japanese partisans, and so on. Everyone struggled to get by, and those with no other resources stitched their living together by selling plastic bottles, nylon socks, and army surplus shoes and clothes, which were valued for their durability. Army "surplus" was the basis of a flourishing black market trade organized by army officers. It left the lowly North Korean foot soldiers wearing threadbare old uniforms and canvas boots that couldn't keep out the rain.

For permission to leave our canton, we had to pull out all the stops. A local pass could be had for a pack of cigarettes and a small quantity of alcohol, but an authorization to move to the

Pyongyang area required much more than that. For a long time our efforts were going nowhere, but a visit from our family changed everything. The Security Force agents, who had been treating our appeals with indifference—not to say contempt—suddenly took an interest in our well-being. They began talking to us and even stopped us in the street to shake our hands! Conditions were evidently ripe for some discreet negotiations. With the aid of a few rather sumptuous gifts—most notably, a Japanese color television—my sister and I were allowed to join our uncle in Pyungsung, a city twenty miles outside Pyongyang. The scientific research center in Pyungsung had requested him to rejoin the post he had held before his internment. As a student at the polytechnic university he had finished first in his class, and his talents were widely recognized. After Yodok, he resumed his chemistry studies, and in 1991 received his doctorate. He was in a good position: the institute's employees were treated as citizens of Pyongyang. It may come as a surprise to some that a former political prisoner was allowed to earn a master's degree and doctorate; but the fact is that my uncle worked in a field where he could be closely monitored and controlled. He also had the benefit of some fabulous luck: the institute's vice-president was his college roommate; and the roommate's uncle, one of Yodok's chief administrators, informed his nephew that the reasons for my uncle's arrest had been minor and that his personal file was clean.

Living in Pyungsung, I was much closer to my mother and able to visit her regularly, sometimes with my sister, but most often alone. We were always happy to see each other. She cooked up little meals for me and bought me clothes. Yet there were a number of things worrying me. Since authorizations for visiting Pyongyang were hard to come by, I often traveled without them, in blatant violation of the law. The community police chief, who was a woman, usually turned a blind eye as long as I came up with a bribe, but how long would she continue before blowing the whistle? I was putting not only myself at risk, but my mother, too. Eventually, I decided to cut back on my visits.

I also had to think about my future. My uncle was pressuring me to enter the university, something my father had always wished. By making the choice now, I would finally obey him. I took the entrance exam, distributed gifts among members of the placement committee, and was accepted to the university for light industry at Hamhung. I would have preferred Pyongyang University, but as a former political prisoner my chances of getting in were close to nil. I attended classes at Hamhung for several months but never found my niche. One problem was that I lived as a boarder in a home to which I had absolutely no connection. The second problem, which eventually proved more debilitating, was the xenophobic atmosphere of that provincial town where "strangers" from other regions were neither liked nor welcomed. To make things worse, the town was full of hoodlums, and I had had quite enough of fighting in the streets. I considered transfering to the university in Pyungsung, but that would have been no easier than getting into Pyongyang. So in the autumn of 1991, I decided to abandon my studies and moved back to our apartment in Pyungsung.

I had to choose a calling outside the university. While I weighed my options, the aid that poured in from my relatives in Japan saved me from poverty. People in the West are familiar with the situation in Cuba, where part of the population subsists on packages sent from family members in the United States and Europe. In North Korea, the manna comes from Japan. The further the North Korean distribution system declines, the more necessary this influx of currency becomes. At the end of the 1980s and the beginning of the 1990s, there were times when even ration tickets—forget about the rations themselves—stopped being distributed. The only way to get anything was by distributing gifts. Fortunately for us, my family was rich enough to earn the friendship both of the county's Party secretary and its manager. The packages and letters from Japan came by mail, via a ship that still makes the fifteen-hour voyage between Niigata and Wonsan once a month. Every package is checked, of course, but only products made in the South are forbidden. Even money is let through. What we needed most, though, was medicine and secondhand clothes.

As far as allowing in visitors, the authorities are of two minds. On the one hand, they are delighted to welcome visitors bearing hard currency. On the other hand, there is always the danger these visitors will disseminate news of the country's troubled political and economic situation. Thus, when a Japanese family comes for a visit, the entire canton is ordered to clean up and look smart. Every village and home that is likely to be seen is swept and improved. Sometimes the authorities go a step further: in advance of our family's arrival, we were moved into a large two-room house, with a shed in the back, so that we might play better hosts. Just before my relatives arrived, Security Force agents dropped by with our orders. We were neither to mention the camp nor complain about anything whatsoever. We could chat, but it was forbidden to mention anything implying criticism of the government. To make sure we obeyed, agents listened in on our conversations around the clock.

By the mid-1980s, after some ten years of protest—much of it from the Chosen Soren—the authorities decided to limit their surveillance to the daytime. Not that it really mattered. If we wanted to have a frank discussion, we only needed to give the agent a little money to go for a walk. . . . The authorities, in any case, really have nothing to fear from visiting relatives—who know the danger they would be putting their family members in if they talked.

열여덟

EIGHTEEN

THE CAMP
THREATENS AGAIN

Around this time, I reestablished contact with my friend Yi Yong-mo—the boy who once became delirious in the middle of class. His family had been released from Yodok four years before we had, but it now looked like they might be on the verge of being sent back. The Security Force had begun calling in his father for interrogations and occasionally summoning my friend as well. We were very close and saw each other often. He told me about his fears and vented his anger against the regime. As a former prisoner, I also was under surveillance, and his friendship could bring me trouble. In the spring of 1991, Yong-mo's father was accused of criticizing Kim Jong-il, and the whole family was sent back to the camp. I haven't heard from my friend since. Is he still alive? He was always a little scrawny, and I fear the worst. . . . He often had fainting spells, during which he broke into a cold sweat. I loved his mind. He was my best and most faithful friend. Apart from my family, there is no one

I miss more. For a time I worried that he would be tortured and made to confess about our counterrevolutionary conversations. In North Korea, every political criminal is tortured: Yong-mo had criticized Kim Jong-il and sung South Korean songs, and for this he was surely beaten and deprived of food and sleep.

I could have continued to live in Pyungsung in relative peace had I not been accused of illegally tuning into South Korean radio. These transmissions I picked up featured songs, covert messages aimed at Party cadres, and analyses of the situation in the North. One program featured interviews with renegades. Another surveyed news from around the world. This was how I learned of the fall and execution of the Ceausescus and of the establishment of diplomatic ties between South Korea and Russia; but it was Nicolae Ceausescu's demise that most impressed me. He was an intimate of Kim Il-sung and had come to visit him many times. I was dying to tell people the news. Was I indiscreet? Perhaps, but I think my real mistake was listening to those programs too often and with too many people. I felt the surveillance of the Security Force gradually tighten around me. The agent who usually took care of my bureaucratic needs in exchange for gifts and loans was avoiding me; worse yet, he wouldn't accept my gifts. Was it now compromising to receive something from my hand? One day, I managed to corner him and get the scoop. "You're under surveillance," he admitted. "A buddy of yours ratted on you for listening to South Korean radio." After making me promise never to reveal my source, he fingered my accuser. I was flabbergasted—it was someone I considered a friend! I never had a clue.

Nothing pleased security agents more than identifying recidivists and sending them back to the camps. Gifts were the only way to keep the agents at bay, and by this point the gifts had to be both lavish and plentiful. How I hated these men. Once I made it to South

Korea, I had no scruples about trying to make their lives as miserable as possible. Whenever I gave interviews, I mentioned how surprised I had been after my denunciation to find myself interrogated by two agents who were my longtime friends and radio-listening companions. I wanted revenge! Those slimeballs probably wound up in the same place they usually sent others. I imagine they've expiated their sins by now, and as far as I'm concerned, they can go free.

In the early 1990s, few North Koreans dared tune in to radio transmissions from the South. Many more do now. I got my two radio receivers from a Pyongyang store where you could get just about anything: cigarettes, beer, clothing, shoes. The only things they didn't have were products made in South Korea—and, of course, they only accepted hard currency. Even foreigners shopped there. Since the sale of radio receivers wasn't as closely monitored as might be expected, I was able to get away with registering one and paying hush money on the second. Listening to South Korean radio had to be done with extreme caution. The poor soundproofing of most North Korean dwellings could easily give us away. To avoid being overheard, my fellow listeners and I took the radio and buried ourselves three or four at a time under a mound of blankets. Only the antenna remained visible.

The other challenge was avoiding static. The signal was always clearest between 11:00 P.M. and 5:00 A.M. We liked listening to the Christian programs on the Korean Broadcasting System. The message of love and respect for one's fellow man was sweet as honey to us. It was so different from what we were used to hearing. In North Korea, the state-run radio and television, newspapers, teachers, and even comic strips only tried to fill us with hate—for the imperialists, the class enemies, the traitors, and who knows what else! We could also tune in to the Voice of America and catch up on the international news from which we had been severed for so long. We hungered for a discourse to break the monopoly of lies. In North Korea, all reality is filtered through a single mind-set. Listening to the radio gave us the words we needed to express our dissatisfaction. Every program, each new discovery, helped us tear a little freer from the enveloping web of deception. Knowledge that there was a counterpoint to official reality was already a kind of escape, one that could exhilarate as well as confuse. It is difficult to explain, for example, the emotions we felt on hearing it demonstrated, proof positive, that the North had actually started the Korean War, not the American imperialists, as we had always been told.

Radio programs from the South made it possible for us to sharpen our criticisms of Kim Il-sung's regime. We had long been aware of all its shortcomings, from corruption to repression, from the camps to food shortages, from its ravishment of the population's work ethic to its obscene wastefulness, most apparent in its sumptuous birthday celebrations in honor of our two idols, father and son. We had plenty of evidence by which to judge the regime—and judge it harshly. What we lacked—what the radio provided us— were the connective elements we needed to tie it all together. The programs furnished us with an overview of the system as a whole: its origins, the reasons behind its current difficulties, the absurdity of its official boasting of self-sufficiency in light of its pleading for international aid. I think my friends and I were proud to be in the know. I wanted very much to tell my uncle about what I had discovered, but I didn't dare; while I knew he would love the South Korean songs, I feared he would forbid me to listen.

There was still a chance my activities might place him at risk, in spite of his ignorance. For everyone's sake, my main objective would have to be parrying as much of the danger as possible. My friend

An-hyuk, who lived in a neighboring county, had also gotten wind of the investigation the Security Force was conducting on me. According to him the agents were proceeding slowly, hoping to throw a dragnet around the entire subculture of illicit auditors. An-hyuk, who also listened to South Korean radio, was facing the same danger I was. Our backs were to the wall: we could either wait for the Security Force to pick us up, or we could try to escape. The options were equally dangerous, but the second presented a glimmer of hope. An-hyuk had sneaked into China once before. On his way back, however, he was arrested for illegal border crossing and sent to Yodok, where he spent the next year and a half. That's how we first met. Later, after we were both released, we kept in touch by mail. It was in one of his carefully coded letters that he revealed that we were in trouble and needed to talk. Our code was simple but effective: we wrote the exact opposite of what we truly meant to say.

In the critical letter, An-hyuk kept repeating that "everything was going really well," that "things were looking up," and so on. He also announced the forthcoming "wedding ceremony of our friends." The reference was oblique, but I understood. We got together and, assessing the situation, agreed we had to escape. But where to? Reaching the South wasn't our primary goal. We simply wanted to avoid the camps any way we could. I had, however, entertained the thought of moving abroad before and had put some money aside for that purpose. The time for action had come; it was almost a question of life and death. If they got us this time, we would be going to a hard-labor camp.

If our plan were to succeed, it would have to remain secret. Even our families would have to be kept in the dark, and telling friends was entirely out of the question. Fortunately, because I was working in the distribution of beans and corn, people were used to seeing me leave town for several days at a time. Our departure thus would not be a cause for immediate suspicion or concern. Questions would eventually arise, of course, but by that time we hoped to be long gone.

It was difficult for me to go this way. I was leaving behind my family and a young girl with whom I was in love. I had met her in Yodok. Her family, who was released when we were, benefited from the aid of a grandmother in Japan. Out of the camp, she had blossomed into a beautiful girl, and I was always thinking about her; yet my shyness and constant moving about made a relationship difficult, and I never declared myself. In the North it's difficult to go steady with a woman, because that sort of intimacy is viewed poorly. So I couldn't even tell her of our plan. What if she turned out to be against it? What if she started telling people?

An-hyuk, for his own part, had been living a relatively happy, independent life for some time, so his parents wouldn't notice his departure for at least a few days. Leaving with him gave me hope. We were friends and trusted each other like brothers. With him by my side, the adventure didn't seem quite so impossible. Had he not already been to China? It's true that he had come back between two border guards, but the experience had surely taught him something. Moreover, a friend of his who had managed a successful escape had let him know that things would be much easier once we were in China.

What I brought to the partnership was a perfect knowledge of the train system and the route to the border zone. In the period following my release from camp, I often took the Pyongyang-Musan line to visit family, who lived up in the north. To avoid any problems—my identification card noted my internment at Yodok—all I had to do was ply the conductors with bribes. When one asked for ID, I told him I didn't have any, but that my parents were Japanese and that I had some yen in my wallet. "I need to travel," I explained, "and if you'll permit, I'll give you what you need." We would go back to his compartment, chat, smoke my Japanese cigarettes. I always dressed impeccably, wearing all-Japanese clothes, and knew exactly how to make the conductor drool: "What else do you need?" I asked. "I'll get it for you next time." It was almost too easy. Rules, however, needed to be observed. I couldn't distribute the gifts haphazardly; they had to be rationed in small, constant doses, so that the receiver would remember and think about them constantly.

I once gave a conductor a Japanese tape recorder. He was very happy, and we began chatting like old friends. When he threatened a woman who was trafficking something, I interceded on her behalf. "She seems really poor," I said. "You should let her be. . . ." And he did. Another conductor, to whom I spoke of my imprisonment, was outraged to learn the cause of my family's travails. But I tried to get him off that line of thinking. It could get dangerous. I said it was just "bad luck; the important thing now is to live well. . . ."

The conductors were generally a corrupt bunch, but that gave them a human side. They were so hungry for our gifts that we could count on them. They always gave perfect advice about who the obliging conductors were on the various trains, in which cars they could be found, and what stations we should pass through. Seiko watches were the most sought-after gifts. My relatives in Japan had brought me about ten of them, enough to satisfy quite a few conductors. I even became friendly with their chief, who told me in advance what number train I should take. He then gave word to his subordinates, so that I would be sure to have no difficulties. Not only would the conductor not check my ticket, he would usually invite me into his compartment so that we might share a drink together. If we craved a snack, he would go out for a food run. Stepping into the neighboring compartment, he would ask, "Who does this package belong to?" A trembling passenger would raise a hand.

"Open it!"

The packages often contained food smuggled in from China.

"Close your eyes, comrade conductor. Take a little for yourself."

The controller would accept his share and bring it back to our compartment so that we might continue with our visit.

Thanks to the money I received from my Japanese relatives, I realized that, despite its uncompromising allegiance to communism, North Korea longed for one thing only: to live as well as Japan. When the country was doing better than it is now—in the 1960s and 1970s, for example—the important thing was to be close to power—and, yes, to wear a Seiko watch. Yet power today is a hollow concept in North Korea. So while the Seiko is still important, most people would rather have a gold ring or a gold tooth than have power. The corruption I have been describing is rather petty. The problem is that it is everywhere, and the higher up you go the less petty it becomes. I once met a former political prisoner who, like many of the wealthy former Japanese residents, had been sent to a camp with his entire family. His father died there. Later, his mother, who was the only descendant of an extraordinarily rich businessman, came into a colossal fortune of some 4 billion yen, or $40 million! The money was deposited into a Chosen Soren bank and largely siphoned off into North Korean coffers, but what remained was enough to transform the family's existence, removing all the obstacles that ordinarily impinge on average North Koreans. After signing a document discouraging her family in Japan from taking legal action against the Chosen Soren, the mother and her family were set free.

Never again would they have to worry about things like traveling papers, because security agents would deliver them right to their door. Agents scurried to them under every imaginable pretext, vying for their little crumb of fortune. My friend's house in Nampo had every Japanese appliance you could think of. And while his family was not allowed to live in Pyongyang, it did own two Toyotas with which to visit the capital. My friend once ran over a group of soldiers while speeding along at seventy miles per hour. He was arrested and sentenced to death, but was released after serving three months in prison! With the aid of refrigerators, color televisions, and bulging envelopes, he was able to bribe the judge and get the case dismissed. In time he grew cynical and contemptuous, and couldn't stand being deprived of anything. He nevertheless did me the honor of keeping me as his friend and was responsible for introducing me to Coca-Cola. That first swallow was simply wonderful. I had a cold. I was cured almost instantly.

열아홉

ESCAPE TO CHINA

I told my family I would be going away for a few days and, on the eve of my departure, informed my girlfriend that I wouldn't see her for a while because of work. I got into a car. The window was slightly open and I stretched out my hand to take hers. I nearly burst into tears. I had lied to her, I was leaving, and she thought I was coming back. It was unbearable. I'm sure she hated me for leaving the way I did, but there was no other way.

I met up with An-hyuk as planned, and we got on the train to Haesan. A few gifts were enough to win over our first conductors, but the controls became stricter and more numerous as we approached the border. The terrain also worked against us: as the train crossed over the northern mountains, the ride became slower and less bumpy, affording the conductors more time to scrutinize identification cards and travel papers. The safest thing for us was to get off before Haesan and walk. It was winter, and at least three feet of snow lay on the ground. We jumped off the train without injury, but the same snow that softened our landing also slowed our progress. In Haesan we stayed three days with a lady friend of An-hyuk who lived alone. An athlete, An-hyuk had contacts throughout the country, mostly people he met in sports clubs. One of his buddies—a boxer—lived in Haesan. He was a smuggler and gang leader, and An-hyuk hoped he might play the middleman in finding us a guide to cross the border. Attempting a crossing alone, without directions or advice, would be far too dangerous. Even if we succeeded in getting to China, we wouldn't know what to do next, except be caught by the Chinese police and sent back to North Korea.

Japsari, the boxer, put us up when we got to Haesan, but he had no interest in helping us find a guide. He spent nearly a week trying to dissuade us from our plan: "An-hyuk tried crossing the border once. He should know what happens to recidivists. If he gets caught, it will be back to camp." Japsari was actually the guy's family name; it meant something like "Eagle Face." He had long, sharply slanted eyes that really did resemble an eagle's. He struck me as a nasty character and I didn't much like him, but I was careful not to let my distrust show. He thought I was the up-and-up type, the kind with whom he could do business. It turned out it was An-hyuk he had reservations about, but there was no question of me leaving without my friend. We talked to him often, sometimes circling our main concern so that we might broach it more forcefully the next time around. In the end, money, beer, and cigarettes got the better of Eagle Face. As he sat fighting sleep at the end of a night of hard drinking, he finally gave a little ground, saying, "One of these days, we'll go do a little tour of China." He kept his word. The next day, he paid some border guards to turn their backs while we made a short round-trip jaunt into China to meet his friend, the guide.

We crossed the Yalu River on foot. Once on the Chinese side, it only took a few minutes to reach the house of the man we hoped would eventually lead us out of the dangerous border zone. After some negotiating, he agreed to take our case and invited us to share a meal with him—which turned out to be an excellent meat dish. His standard of living was palpably superior to ours. He was a young man, between twenty-two and twenty-five years old, a Chinese citizen of Korean ancestry who made his living by cross-border trading, importing deer antlers and ginseng from North Korea and exporting socks, sweaters, and scarves back across. It was a profitable business, because Chinese goods are expensive in the North. He was proud of his work and told us he had already put aside 50,000 yuan and had another 50,000 entrusted to a well-connected North Korean businessman charged with pouncing on any good deals that might come his way. Our guide avoided overtly illegal dealings, declared his merchandise, and obtained official North Korean travel permits whenever possible. Surprisingly, North Korea charges no customs on imported products. The border guards search for illegal materials such as subversive or pornographic literature, but they don't tax common goods. I don't know how else North Korea would get by; apart from the Party cadres, who dress in Japanese clothes, everyone wears Chinese-made garments, if they can afford anything at all. Taxes are charged on goods entering China, but they can be avoided by buying off a head border guard with alcohol, cigarettes, or clothing. In exchange, the guard will allow you to enter the country without crossing the bridge. The smuggling occurs practically out in the open. Every frontier town in North Korea has middlemen. Their "imported" merchandise so overpacks the trains that it often causes accidents. The merchants don't even need traveling papers to cross the border, because a little money will do just fine in their stead. It's clear: North Korea is a total sham. Officially, it outlaws private business, but in the shadows it lets it thrive. Since there are hardly any markets, merchants warehouse their Chinese products at home and sell them to their neighbors and acquaintances. This farce is the only thing preventing the bankruptcy of the North Korean state and the pauperization of its citizenry.

We arrived back at the Korean bank of the river at the appointed hour and saw Japsari's purchased guards miraculously walk off in the opposite direction, just as planned. We remained on the riverbank for a while to case the guard posts and observe the guard rotation schedule. Our guide said that at certain times the watchmen left their stations to give various traffickers and smugglers a chance to get across. We stayed in Korea for another few days with a friend of Japsari's who was extremely welcoming—largely because he thought he could hitch me to his sister-in-law. Marriage, however, was the last thing on my mind. On the agreed-upon night, we headed off toward the Yalu.

It was 2:00 A.M. The night was black, without moon or stars. We found our trail but had difficulty following it in the pitch dark. Finally, we reached the riverbank. With the temperature around 0°F, the Yalu—or the Amnok, as we Koreans call it—was covered in a thick sheet of ice. As I began to cross, I was overtaken by an intense whirl of emotions that had nothing to do with fear. Images of my family forced their way into my consciousness: I saw my mother, my sister, my aunts and uncles. Questions began shooting through my mind: Would I ever see them again? Would I ever be able to return to this country? I suddenly felt very anxious. I was standing before the *River of No Return*. . . . I stopped in my tracks for a moment, then bowed my head and went on.

The river crossing didn't take long, two minutes, perhaps, of running across the ice with as little noise as possible. I still remember clearly the mix of emotions I felt just then. There was certainly fear— of getting caught and of what awaited me on the other side—but I also felt sadness. I was abandoning something indefinable that was reproaching me for leaving. . . . Those two or three minutes on the ice were like an eternity.

Though the area was supposed to be under surveillance, we didn't see a single guard. Running across the border today is even easier: many more people are at the starting line, and the guards are more lax than ever. Just give them some money or a good pack of cigarettes and they'll let you pass. Back in 1992, if they saw a fugitive, they would cry "Halt," then start firing.

We arrived at our guide's house tired and out of breath. We found him dressed in South Korean–made jacket and pants, which must have cost the equivalent of a North Korean worker's monthly wages. He was a man bubbling over with plans, the first of which was to move to South Korea as soon as he had enough money saved up. "Going from the North directly to the South is impossible," he said with effect, trying to bait us. But we weren't going for it. We had taken the precaution of not telling him we were wanted by the authorities. While he was happy to help people make little "business" trips into China, he had no interest in running seriously afoul of the law. To help ensure he kept quiet about our crossing, I gave him a handsome wad of cash, for which he was also supposed to find us a truck to Yonji—or Yongil, as we say in Korea—the capital of China's autonomous Korean region. As we sat chatting that first night, we heard some astonishing things from our guide. We learned, for example, that he was actually a member of the Chinese Communist Party. It was totally baffling. Korean Communists were hard, austere ideologues—or at least tried to act that way—and here was this Chinese Communist proudly flaunting his wealth!

The next evening's meal was as ample as the first. The guide's wife claimed it was just the usual fare, but what was ordinary to them was gargantuan to me: there were many different dishes, and several had meat! I couldn't believe my eyes. I felt as if I'd been invited to a feast for Party cadres. In the North, alcohol is very expensive; an average bottle sells for 10 won, one-tenth of a worker's monthly wages. The most popular spirit, *paï jou* (white alcohol), comes from China. It costs 60 won a bottle and is usually reserved for special occasions. Here it was being poured into our glasses as an ordinary accompaniment to an improvised meal! To get an idea of the Korean standard of living, it's worth noting that on the black market, 150 won buys $2 U.S.—the official rate is 15 won to the dollar—which is one-and-a-half times an ordinary worker's monthly salary, or exactly enough to buy one pack of Marlboro cigarettes. With that as my point of reference, China was like paradise, and I began to sense the huge gulf separating the universe as I knew it and the world as it might actually be.

There were more surprises to come. After dinner, our host suggested we walk to a nightclub in the neighboring village. We accepted the invitation—though I couldn't help thinking, Don't these people go to work? It was nearing midnight, and we were only now stepping out! Finally, I worked up the courage to ask, "Don't you have to wake up early tomorrow?" His answer left me stunned: it was "up in the air!" His next observation, though, is the one that really did me in. "In any case," he said, "the important thing isn't work; it's to enjoy life." I was speechless.

We walked to the next village, which was called Changbaekhyun in Korean. All along the main street, people stood out on their front stoops, talking and laughing. The streets were brightly lit, neon signs glowing. Across the river, on the Korean bank, everything was still, enveloped in darkness. The river separated two worlds. On one side, North Korea, "calm as hell," as we say here, and on the other, the loud, luminous paradise. We stepped into an establishment where people stood drinking around a dance floor while couples slowly swayed to the music, holding each other close. I stared, wide-eyed. I'm sure I looked very out of place, but nothing like the unfortunate renegades one sees in that village today—haggard, thin, poorly dressed, and fleeing famine. My departure had been well organized; I wore Japanese clothes and looked more elegant than most of the Chinese people around me. A young lady came up to ask me for a dance. I was embarrassed and declined her invitation, explaining that I didn't know how. "That doesn't matter," she said, smiling. "I'll show you." I continued to demur. Disappointed, she left before I could change my mind. So I was now in a country where the women asked the men? Things were moving faster than I could keep pace. No girl in North Korea would dare make such a proposition. The young lady was very pretty, and I would have loved to have danced with her. I declined not only because I didn't know how to dance, but because I was overwhelmed. I watched as she sauntered over to a nearby table, where the next man accepted her offer. They danced and I watched, regretting my awkwardness and timidity.

I started in on another drink, trying to unwind. An-hyuk and our guide were deep in conversation. A feeling of great joy suddenly swept over me, a sentiment akin to hope. Here was life. . . . I felt as though I wanted to throw my arms around it, to embrace it as I should have done with that young lady. I was sure I was going to live and encounter other chances. I was light-headed and felt something heavy and dull swell inside me like a wave. It was close to 1:00 A.M. when we left the club. Our guide walked us around the village, holding forth about recent changes in local commerce. We even discussed the general economic situation. I couldn't believe it: in the North, such freedom of speech is inconceivable. Citizens there feel they're under constant surveillance—which for the most part, they are. The monitoring is systematic. When it's not your identification card they ask for, it's your traveling papers. "In China," said our host, "as long as you don't oppose the Party openly or act too suspiciously, you can do as you like. . . ."

It took me a long time to fall asleep that night. Images of the North and of my family paraded through my mind, punctuated by snapshots of the young Chinese woman who had asked me to dance. I began to wonder if I would ever meet her again and whether I would ever overcome my shyness. I felt like laughing: my first night out of North Korea, and here I was worried about how best to comport myself on the dance floor! This wasn't how I imagined my escape.

The next night we made the journey to Yonji with our guide, trundling over mountain roads until the wee hours of the morning. Though we were already in March, the temperature was down around –5°F—which was not unusual for the mountainous region where many of the passes rise above six thousand feet. Arriving at our destination stiff and chilled to the bone, our guide took us to the home of his sister, who lived with her husband and mother-in-law. The extended family, which was also of Korean ancestry, gave us a warm welcome and offered to lodge us for a time.

We nevertheless began to worry for our safety. I was growing suspicious of our guide, a Communist Party member who had worked hard to cultivate a reputation for meticulous legality. We also made a decision to tell our hosts, who inspired in us great confidence, the real reason behind our voyage to China. It was during dinner that I let slip the truth.

"We have something important to tell you," I began. "We are neither tourists nor merchants. We're on the run and have no intention of going back to North Korea. Life there is very hard, and we are wanted by the police for having listened to South Korean radio."

They asked us where we intended to go next.

"We don't really know," I said. "Japan, or maybe the United States. . . ."

"Why not to the South?" they asked. "We've heard that life isn't bad there."

Sure, why not, but how could we get there? And how could we explain our inherent fear of the South, instilled in us by a lifetime of propaganda? It was tempting, though—another taboo to break. What resistance we still had was much weakened by our hosts' manner of taking the South's superiority so completely for granted. Yet, when our guide discovered our true reasons for crossing the Yalu, he wanted nothing more to do with us.

"I don't want to get mixed up in this," he raged. "If you don't go back to the North right away, I'm turning you in!"

His relatives intervened on our behalf and got him to calm down. Having twice given him fifty dollars—hefty sums by Chinese standards—I thought he was being very ungrateful. With tempers still running high, he headed back home, and to this day I don't know whether or not he denounced us.

An-hyuk and I were scared. We wanted to get away that very night, but to where? We didn't speak Chinese or even know exactly where in the country we were. Yet all was not lost. We had our hosts, as well as a friend of our guide, a wealthy Yonji merchant who invited us out to a karaoke club.

"Come on, you're not risking a thing," he said. "No one ever gets their papers checked. The police are on the club's payroll: they never bother anyone."

It was my first time in such a place. An-hyuk and I sat down feeling very timid and ill at ease. The young Chinese women who served the drinks gave us very suggestive glances, which made me tremble slightly. The behavior of the Chinese men, too, was both fascinating and shocking. How could they kiss and caress these girls in front of everyone without feeling embarrassed? I was jarred by a China so willing to make a spectacle of itself. Crossing the Yalu River wasn't enough to flush out the propaganda seeped into us over so many years. I began to wonder whether the North Korean authorities weren't justified in fearing capitalism's nefarious influence on China! But I think what scared me was the prospect of enjoying life. The ideas to which I had sworn allegiance since youth—work, discipline, devotion to the Party and its Guide—were making their last stand.

All around me people laughed; the bottles and glasses passed from hand to hand; the girls were nice without being vulgar. Little by little, I began to relax. Soon we were drinking and singing with a couple of girls who mistook us for South Koreans. To make us happy, they regaled us with songs from Seoul, closing their private performance with "You Can't Imagine How Much I Love You," a hit by the ever-popular Petty Kim. Her ex-husband, who was a composer, wrote the tune for her after her remarriage to a rich Italian.

A few days after our karaoke night, the merchant told us that our guide had strongly advised him that, unless he wanted to compromise his social position, he would do well to put us aside. The man clearly liked us, but it was equally clear he would be relieved to see us go. Another denunciation was definitely something we could do without. We thus resolved to push our plans forward and, a few evenings later, took our leave of the home that had so hospitably taken us in. We spent our first night sleeping under the stars, but we couldn't do that forever. Bum around long enough, and we'd be sure to arouse suspicion. So the next day we walked over to another of our guide's relatives, a woman whose house on the outskirts of Yonji would have been a perfect hideout. At first, she was afraid our presence might bring her family trouble. Yet she was convinced of our honesty and felt sympathy for our fate, and in the end she relented to our pleading and allowed us to stay with her a night or two, just long enough to buy train tickets for Shenyang—or Moukden, as it was called during the Manchurian dynasty—where An-hyuk had a friend.

The ride from Yonji to Shenyang lasted about ten hours, during which we felt very vulnerable and alone. When a conductor approached us, I went pale. I was afraid he was asking me for my transit papers; but that wasn't it. Our neighbor, who spoke Korean, explained that he wanted to see our tickets. We handed them over, still trembling, forgetting to breathe until he was gone. Compared to North Korea, we were traveling in a free country. In the North, not speaking the language would have been enough to render us immediately suspect. I had heard there was freedom of movement in China, but to actually experience it was another matter altogether! Relieved and newly confident, we abandoned ourselves to sleep.

We arrived in Shenyang in the dark, early morning hours. We felt bitterly cold and as worried and tense as ever. We were all alone in a city we could barely find on a map, ignorant of the language, and unaware of the police's habits. In the Korean-speaking province, apart from the karaoke episode, it was possible to forget we were in a foreign country. We now had the impression of truly being in another world. Even the buildings looked different. The large, teeming city intimidated us. We felt as if we'd crossed some other, invisible border. I was getting the jitters. I felt abandoned in an immense world, an orphan for all time. I could die now and no one would know. Fortunately, there were two of us. A few schoolboy jokes were enough to revive our spirits. What we really needed to do, however, was stop wandering the streets. It was too dangerous: police were about, and they occasionally checked the IDs of passersby. We managed to avoid them, but decided it would be safer to step into a movie house until dawn. The first theater we happened on was showing a Hong Kong kung fu film. We took our seats, exhausted, and fell asleep almost immediately. After the show, we somehow found our way to the home of An-hyuk's friend, a guy he had met on his first visit to China. We arrived at his place between 7:30 and 8:00 A.M. He was half asleep when he opened the door. He was hardly able to believe his eyes.

"An-hyuk, what are you doing here?"

They hugged each other, and the man asked us in. Then we got another surprise: he had a woman with him.

"You're married?" An-hyuk asked.

"No, she's just a good friend. We live together."

In North Korea, it's not possible for an unmarried couple to live together. The young man spoke of love, but An-hyuk and I found the situation scandalous and quickly changed the subject. We told him our story, and he agreed to put us up for a while, then escort us to the South Korean consulate in Beijing. After a month of postponements, we finally set out on the seven-hour train ride.

The Chinese capital impressed me as more Western and capitalist than specifically Chinese. Most striking were the billboards for Daewoo, Samsung, and Lucky Star, all featuring both Chinese characters and Latin script. South Korea may be a small country, I thought, but it seems to reign supreme in China. It was a shocking sight for someone who had grown up on doomsday depictions of a country rife with strikes, where legions of poor workers struggled desperately to survive from one economic crisis to the next. . . . I was also impressed by the width of the streets and the cleanliness of a city that was livelier and more modern than Shenyang.

Behind the big buildings and commercial advertisements, certain aspects of a more traditional China still held fast. Take the public bathrooms, for example. I remember my first experience with one of them: on opening the door, I found myself face to face with people squatting next to one another, chatting and reading their newspapers as they relieved themselves; I quickly closed the door. Was I dreaming? No partitions, no flush chains. Even in the camp, we had partitions and swinging doors to give us a little privacy! The public bathrooms would turn out to be one of the most difficult aspects of our sojourn; all the toilets we encountered followed the same basic model. Since I absolutely needed to go, I waited discreetly at the exit until the bathroom was nearly empty before entering.

Our reason for coming to Beijing was not tourism, however, and we quickly left the station and flagged down a taxi. As we climbed in, An-hyuk's friend nonchalantly commanded the chauffeur: "To the Korean consulate." We arrived about fifteen minutes later. Just as we were stepping out of the car, we realized there had been a serious misunderstanding. We were standing in front of the North Korean embassy! We turned tail and hailed another taxi. The South Korean consulate turned out to be the second floor of an ordinary-looking building. Upon entering the office, we were greeted by a young woman, who smiled at us from behind her reception desk.

"Hello," I said. "We've come from the North."

Her smile went suddenly flat, and she scurried off toward the back to tell someone about our arrival. She returned followed by a man, who politely invited us into a large office. A South Korean flag hung from one of the walls. My feelings were powerfully confused: I was face to face with both the diabolical South and the longed-for end of my journey. The world had turned inside out. We told the man our story, and he took notes, neither making comments nor asking questions. Something about him struck me as too calm. I tried not to let my feelings show, but I was choking with indignation: we had come so far, traversed so many dangers, and none of it seemed of much weight to this man. Not only did he appear untouched by our suffering, he seemed skeptical of our story's veracity. I had hoped the consulate would be willing to hide and protect us, but that, it turned out, was out of the question. The diplomat gave us a bit of pocket money, wished us luck, and bid us to come to see him in a couple of weeks. In the meantime, he would see what he could do for us. . . . Before we could respond, we were being led out to the staircase. Returning two weeks later, we were once again counseled to have patience. I felt more and more alone and realized that my life shouldn't depend on anyone, not even a representative of the country I wished to join.

From a human rights perspective, my case was shocking. Yet how many people really care about the fate of a refugee lost in China? Like every government in the world, the South Korean government acts on the basis of national interests. The way it handles refugee matters is no exception. Yet, to consider the plight of refugees exclusively as a matter of national interest amounts to neglecting the rights of individuals. In Seoul, many years later, I ran into the same diplomat who had received me so coldly. "You must realize," he began by way of apology, "that establishing our burgeoning diplomatic relations with China had taken us a very long time and required enormous efforts. We simply could not allow ourselves to act in a manner that would place China in an embarrassing situation vis-à-vis its ally in the North. . . ."

After coming up empty at the South Korean consulate, we returned to Shenyang with An-hyuk's friend. Something in his attitude, however, had begun to change. He was becoming colder, more aloof. Our suspicion grew when he suggested we address our case to the Chinese authorities. He said that doing so might allow us to obtain a residency authorization and prevent us from being stopped without papers. Perhaps, but it was well known at the time that the North Korean government offered substantial gifts—color television sets, for example—to anyone who offered key assistance in the repatriation of its refugees. One little tip to the higher-ups at the Shenyang Association for Chinese of Korean Ancestry—which was controlled by Pyongyang—and we would be picked up and whisked across the border. To buy ourselves a little time, we thought it wise to offer An-hyuk's friend a wad of yens and let him understand that more might be coming. Three days later, we left for the city of Dalian—formerly known as Dairen—the Chinese port closest to South Korea.

스물

SMALL-TIME
PROSTITUTION AND
BIG-TIME SMUGGLING
IN DALIAN

One Sunday we stepped out for what we said was a little walk, leaving behind a few of our things to lend our lie some credibility. The train ride to Dalian passed without incident, but we had no definite plan besides avoiding police patrols and eating. In the meantime, blending into a crowd and getting some food seemed like a fine idea, so we headed for the market. It must have been around 1:00 P.M. The streets were peopled but far from packed. Dalian doesn't really liven up until evening, when its streets metamorphose into an immense bazaar, brimming with every manner of food and clothing merchant. We were strolling through the market like tourists, considering what our next step might be, when suddenly we heard Korean. Next to us, three women were chatting it up. It was as though a lifesaver had been thrown our way. I grabbed it without thinking. One of them seemed particularly nice. She was around thirty, well-dressed.

"*Onni*,"* I asked, "are you Korean?"

She answered my question with another question.

"Where are you from?"

I decided to go for it.

"From the North," I told her. "We've hit a rough spot. Could you help us?"

She gave us a close once-over, dismissed her friends, then led us to a nearby restaurant and ordered us *bulgogi*—a kind of Korean barbecue—with rice and beer.

"Alright," she said once we were settled, "let's hear your story."

She sat listening to us for a long time, occasionally nodding her head to encourage us to continue. She was visibly moved, but afterward the only thing she would reveal about herself was that her parents were also from North Korea and that she had no sympathies for Kim Il-sung—we could be quite sure of that. By the time we ended our meal, she had invited us to stay with her. Her apartment was large and messy. And we were bewildered to find it inhabited by about fifteen young women, most of them around twenty years old and several of them Korean. It didn't take much to figure out they were prostitutes, living there under the protection of our new friend, who also lodged her adoptive niece.

I am indebted to all those women for one of the most important times in my life. A current of sympathy ran among us, growing stronger with time. Our hostess, whom I will call Madame Yi, eventually proposed that she and I join in an oath to make us like brother

---

*Literally, "older sister," a respectful form of address employed regardless of any actual family connection.

and sister. I was deeply moved and accepted immediately. From that point forward, our mutual affection would be unconditional, vulnerable only to death. Once our pact was sealed, I was allowed to discover that, aside from her escort service, this energetic woman also ran another business, whose secrecy was more scrupulously maintained. Most of her earnings came from smuggling snakes into South Korea, where they are a rare and highly prized delicacy. I had eaten them myself at Yodok, but that was only because I was dying of hunger. As far as I knew, there was no shortage of food in the South! Madame Yi laughed at my naivete and explained that virility-obsessed South Koreans ate snakes for the supposed aphrodisiacal virtues they shared with eel, ginseng, deer antlers, bear bile, and, of course, seal's penis—the be-all and end-all of sexual aids.

Madame Yi bought the reptiles from a network of local roughnecks who caught them in the mountains. She had a warehouse not far from her apartment where she kept the snakes until she could arrange transport—she had her connections—aboard a South Korea–bound ship. The most difficult part of the affair was keeping the snakes in their boxes until shipping time: they could slip through the smallest of holes. The police already had been called out once by frightened neighbors and needed to be paid off with money and girls. Madame Yi bought the snakes for less than 100 yuan and resold them to specialized dealers for $10 apiece. With two deliveries a month, each of one thousand snakes, it was a highly lucrative business.

An-hyuk and I played it safe and went out as little as possible. Our hostess advised us to keep a low profile, though she was equally worried we might be turned in by one of her employees, a girl whose father was none other than president of the Association of Koreans in Dalian. Madame Yi had little cause for concern though:

the girl was not only the prettiest of the bunch, she was the most generous, too. She had fallen in love with An-hyuk and took meticulous care of him when he fell ill. Neither did she hesitate to dip into her own nest egg to help us. With several Pyongyang agents among her clients, she even promised to warn us if she ever got wind of impending danger. I had such trust in her that I told her my real name. If she wanted to turn me in, so be it. Perhaps it's naive, but I've always had the belief that women would shield and protect me from the vicissitudes of fate.

After a month in Dalian, I offered to work for my hostess. I didn't want to continue living off her good graces. She refused at first, saying that as long as I was in China, I was her guest; my turn to help her out would come one day, too. I insisted so much, though, she finally started giving me odd jobs around the snake warehouse. A little later, when she needed a discreet, reliable assistant, she chose me. As for the girls, they generally hung around the apartment, joking and flirting with us until a customer called. At night they went out to the docks. When they met someone they didn't mind spending some time with, they asked him for a little present.

One night, one of them told me a North Korean navy ship had pulled into port. Having by this time grown less timid, An-hyuk and I decided to check it out, taking four girls along for company. Down by the docks we walked up to several sailors and stared in mock wonderment at the Kim Il-sung badges attached to their uniforms.

"Are you from the North?" I asked in Korean. "We're Chinese of Korean descent. I even lived in the North for a while."

Delighted at meeting semicompatriots, they all shook our hands. I was finding the situation rather amusing. They wanted to do some shopping and were very happy when we offered to lend our assistance. The ubiquitous security agent who was accompanying them—a typical specimen you could spot a mile away—made no objection. An-hyuk, the girls, and I thus became their negotiators and interpreters for the day, walking them through the market's maze of streets and alleyways and letting them sense that our company was winning them discounts. The whole thing struck me as very funny. I felt euphoric, like I could do anything. I even had the gumption to draw the sailors into a conversation about the state of affairs in North Korea.

"I'm not sure Kim Il-sung is as good a leader as you claim he is," I ventured.

They tripped over one another running to his defense.

"How dare you say that?" they asked. "What do you have against him?"

I limited my observations to the country's economic difficulties. They responded that the troubles were of a passing nature, brought on by Russia having stabbed communism in the back and broken off economic relations with the North. The country would soon get back on its feet, though; they were as sure of this as of their Great Leader, Kim Il-sung. But as soon as the security agent went to the bathroom, one of the sailors admitted he agreed with me. He wore the Kim Il-sung badge because he had to, not because he supported the regime.

"You and your friends would do well to take them off," I told him, "at least while you're doing your shopping. The Chinese take North Koreans for dupes and jack up the prices on them. . . ."

An-hyuk and I were giddy with malice.

The soldiers held a hushed discussion among themselves, then did as I suggested. Poor wretches! They had no more than a dollar or two to their name. It was sad to look at them. I don't even know how much I spent that day helping them buy socks, belts, and other knickknacks. Dazzled by the abundance of merchandise, they couldn't stop singing China's praises. In the end, I made them another proposition.

"If you have a little money left over, I can set you up with a pretty girl."

"How much?" they asked.

"200 yuan."

"Okay," they said. "That'll be for next time."

They were fascinated by the girls' miniskirts. I had the same reaction at first. But I had gotten used to it.

Weeks passed, then months. Madame Yi suggested several times that I settle down in Dalian. Her niece, she said, would be happy to be my wife. That we got on well was true, and my life in that city was certainly agreeable. Kim Yong-sun, the niece, waited on me hand and foot, and she had presented me to her family, who invited me over regularly. Before long I was being received like a regular fiancé. A consummate matchmaker, Madame Yi often organized outings for us. We would catch a ferry out to one of the islands off Dalian, stopping to eat mussels and taking long walks. Those were beautiful days, and they showed me I was as capable of enjoying life as my fellow humans.

Madame Yi's offer was tempting, but I felt I hadn't yet come to the end of my journey. South Korea attracted me more than ever. During my time in Dalian, I learned more about the country. I had heard it was richer than China and incomparably more democratic. My curiosity was piqued. After ten years in Yodok, I also felt an obligation to the people I'd left behind. I had to expose the existence of these camps, to denounce the way North Korea's population was being walled in, surveyed, and punished under the slightest pretext. I had to tell my grandfather's story. In South Korea this would be most possible.

Moreover, I still had reason to fear being stopped by a police patrol and getting sent back to where I'd come from. Despite my relative contentment, it was time to go. As Madame Yi's contraband business proved, finding passage was not impossible. Perhaps I could even trade places with a few snakes and sneak into Korea among a shipment of precious aphrodisiacs. Madame Yi laughed at my suggestion, but after much prodding, she agreed to help me secure passage. We kept Kim Yong-sun in the dark. She would have wept and made a scene, insisting I take her along, which was impossible. I'm sad when I think about it now and feel awful about the way I treated her—especially considering how she once saved me from a police patrol on the train from Dalian to Beijing.

Toward the end of July 1992, Madame Yi began sending out feelers for a ship to carry An-hyuk and me to the South. Most of the captains she spoke to considered it too risky and were unwilling to run afoul of the Chinese authorities for our sake. After meeting with countless refusals, she finally aroused the interest of a captain with whom she'd had previous dealings and who was a regular visitor to her girls. The money involved, however, was not enough to allay all his fears. His ship sailed under a Honduran banner, the accepted practice among ships running between China and South Korea prior to the opening of the countries' official diplomatic relations on August 24, 1992. His good-sized freighter transported various merchandise, including cereals, sesame seeds, beans, and dried seafood. Humans were not usually part of the cargo. Since he really didn't know us, he looked to Madame Yi for reassurance.

"If I do this, will it be good or bad?" he asked.

"It will be good for the country, good for peace, and—most importantly—you'll save these two young people's lives."

The deal was sealed without further ado.

스물하나

ARRIVAL IN
SOUTH KOREA

Our departure was set for September 14. The captain planned everything in great detail, because carrying it out wouldn't be easy. To get to the ship, we would need to cross a bridge that spanned an arm of the sea. All along the bridge were stationed Chinese police and customs officers. Fortunately, "Honduran" crews were treated with relative laxity, their papers receiving only perfunctory examination. When our captain's men went broadside for drinks, he borrowed two of their IDs for An-hyuk and me, and also picked us up some sailor clothes. It was time to head for the ship.

The captain walked ahead with us close on his heels. I looked straight in front of me and forced a smile, but my heart was beating through my shirt and my legs felt like rubber. It only took thirty seconds to cross the bridge, but it seemed an eternity. I tried to show my card as quickly and nonchalantly as possible, but one of the policemen bent forward, apparently trying to get a better look. I almost

217

passed out. I knew I was wavering between life and death. I no longer saw the turnstile ahead, and I felt like I had entered a movie that was in slow motion. But the policeman seemed to lose his train of thought. For no reason I could see, he suddenly straightened up and looked past our group. My wobbly legs resumed their march. My head felt completely empty, weightless. . . . Thinking back on it, I'm sure that policeman was not the least bit interested in either me or the photo. At the time, though, I thought the game was up.

Once we were on the ship, the next step was finding a place to hide. An hour before a ship's departure for another country, Chinese police come aboard to check for clandestine passengers. They count the sailors, double-check their IDs, and search the ship from bow to stern. To avoid discovery, An-hyuk and I slipped into the heating oil tank, where we waded up to our hips in unctuous liquid. Only the captain and the lieutenant knew we were on board. We stayed down there for three hours, enveloped in the din of machinery and breathing in noxious fumes, until the ship finally pulled out of Chinese territorial waters. After luxuriating in a series of long showers to wash out the smell of oil, we went up on deck. We were approaching the end of our journey. As when crossing the Yalu River, again I was assailed by memories of my family and my connections to the North. I was worried that Japanese or Korean papers might write about my case. What then would happen to my family? I tried to take comfort in the fact that whatever damage there might be was probably already done. There was no turning back. And I'd won on at least two counts: I was safe and sound, and I would be able to tell the world about life in the North Korean camps.

When we finally reached international waters, the captain put out a call to all South Korean ships in the vicinity. He thought this would be less dangerous than trying to land us in Japan—his first port of call—though there was a chance his radio appeal could be intercepted by a North Korean vessel. Shortly after the message was sent, we saw a military ship approach. Day had turned to night by then and it was difficult to identify its markings. Was it from the North or the South? Our anxiety rose. After pulling to within a few dozen yards, the ship suddenly switched on its searchlights and trained them directly on us. Someone then got on the loudspeaker and demanded that our ship stop and identify itself. It was the South Korean ship we had called for! A couple of their sailors were invited aboard to speak with our captain in private. When they were done, the South Korean sailors signaled for us to follow them back to their ship. We thanked our smuggler with great emotion, tears in our eyes. The man had saved our lives.

Once on board, the captain of the South Korean vessel asked us a few brief questions—age, name, profession. He wrote down our responses, then relayed them to Seoul via radio. We were then taken to a cabin that looked like a fancy hotel room, color television included. All evening officers came around to meet us, offer words of encouragement, and ask about our plans. The warmth of our reception took us aback. We had long since weaned ourselves from the force-fed lies of the North, but such geniality on the part of "puppets of American imperialism" nevertheless was hard to fathom. We were later joined by the ship's captain, who wanted to question us further about our itinerary, the places where we had lived, our work and professional training. Afterward, we followed his suggestion to try to rest and relax. We turned on South Korean television for the first time in our lives.

Suddenly, the program we were watching was interrupted for a special bulletin: two young men from North Korea were on their way to the South after having passed through a "third country"—as China was conventionally called. Once the surprise passed, we savored uncensored television, surfing channels and sampling various programs. We had a minder with us in the cabin, a young man who was doing his obligatory military service, but his presence was not in the least oppressive. The voyage was pleasant, with calm seas and generous blue skies. Food was brought to our cabin, and between meals, we were served snacks of beer and cake.

At one point the ship stopped for several hours. I imagine it was awaiting word from Seoul about how to proceed. If so, the orders finally came and, three hours later, as night was falling, we arrived at the military port of Inchon, not far from Seoul. There were many soldiers waiting for us at the docks, along with several men in civilian clothing—South Korean security agents, no doubt. They took An-hyuk and me by the arms and led us into separate cars. I sat in the middle of the backseat with a burly guard on either side. We drove off toward Seoul, stopping at an ordinary-looking detached house. A lavish spread was waiting for us on the dining-room table, and before moving on to serious business, we were invited to indulge. Afterward, An-hyuk and I were taken to separate rooms and given long interrogations. The agents apparently wanted to make sure our stories jibed. They asked me the same question over and over again. At one point, the agent who was interrogating me said, "You see, I've asked you this question three times in three different ways, and each time you've given me exactly the same answer. If you're lying, you're very smart about it!" He handed me a sheet of paper and asked me to draw a map of Yodok. I did as I was told, trying to remember every detail and devoting particular attention to Ipsok, the executions site, and to the mountains. The agent seemed a little surprised. He gave me a long look, then pulled a photograph out of his desk drawer. I couldn't believe my eyes: it was my camp! Spotting my hut, I let out a cry. The agent lowered his head. He was beginning to trust me. I then identified the other structures for him: the bachelor's barracks, the distillery. . . . This went on for a quite a while. I told him everything I knew. The atmosphere in the room had changed completely since the start of the questioning. The agent was relaxed, his forced geniality had turned to genuine good humor, and I confided in him with perfect trust. The debriefing lasted a week. It was conducted by two agents who relieved each other at two-hour intervals. If I needed a break, I could go to sleep in an adjoining room. Then we'd start in again. The agents stayed in the building around the clock, just like me.

At the end of that week, I was allowed to leave the office. Though the interrogation had left me feeling dazed and empty, I understood why my story interested the authorities and thought it normal that they wanted to confirm its veracity. Though the interrogation was over, I continued to live in the same house and to take my meals with the security agents and their directors. At the end of the first week, the head of the security service came up to shake my hand.

"You've cleared the first hurdle," he said. "But there will be others. You've come from a long way off, you know. . . ." He paused, then concluded with a note of particular sincerity: "Of all the renegades I've met, you have suffered among the most."

In time, my interaction with the agents grew less formal and my schedule less constricted. The process lasted approximately six months. The subsequent interrogations—or conversations, really—became progressively shorter and less frequent. The questions shifted from the camp to my years in the Yodok *gun* and my work in distribution. I also gave many interviews and began to study English as a diversion. After the initial interrogation, I was also allowed to spend time with An-hyuk. We'd sit around chatting, smoking cigarettes, and reading the day's paper. At the end of three months, we were moved into the same room.

Our initial anxieties—after twenty-five years in North Korea, it's no small matter to be moved into a South Korean security office—lessened. The even-tempered agents never ceased to astonish me. They were made of different stuff than the ones I had encountered in the North. One of my two interrogators in particular seemed to develop a strong liking for me. He often brought me a book, some money, or a little something special to eat. Even if it was part of his job, a true bond developed, a bond of man to man. We've remained friends to this day. In time, I was granted authorization to leave the interrogation center—with a companion, of course. He showed me the famous sites of Seoul: City Hall, Namdaemun, the banks of the Han River, the parks, Itaewon. One evening, we went up the Namsam Television Tower and saw all of Seoul lit up below us. The view filled me with wonder.

What most struck me, however, was the way people led their lives. Everyone seemed free to do as they wished. No system organized their movements and activities. I have to admit that it rather worried me at first. This sort of society just couldn't last; it could never face a crisis. I later realized that this only seemed like disorder. A pervading logic governed peoples' interactions. Though the principle of everybody for himself reigned supreme, people here appeared honest; they thought about others and shared common values. Seoul was teeming with cars. I'd never seen so many. I was amazed to learn that most of them were actually manufactured in Korea itself. This was never mentioned in the North. I remember the pride I felt at this discovery—my first feeling of pride for South Korea. I eventually became enamored of that sprawling city, with its millions of inhabitants, its forest of modern skyscrapers, its dense traffic, its bustling life and nocturnal energy.

Whenever a renegade arrives in Seoul, a press conference is called. Our case was no exception. A month after our arrival, we were brought to the Seoul Press Center to be interviewed by several dozen journalists. They began with typical questions about how we made it to South Korea, life in the camp, and so forth. But then they turned to the agents to inquire when and how we were found, what instructions we had been given prior to this interview, and whether we had been guaranteed freedom of speech. It was a terrible shock. I had been through so many awful things, and these people, who had lived their whole lives swaddled in perfect comfort, were looking skeptically down their noses at me! Clearly, my address was unfavorable to the North. Clearly, our testimony about the camps and the repressiveness of the Pyongyang regime would bolster the South's claim that it was the legitimate representative of the Korean nation. But so what? Did telling the truth necessarily mean having to oppose the government? Was I supposed to declare I had been manipulated by the South's Security Service? Was the capitalist South always supposed to be in the wrong?

I found the journalist from the newspaper *Hangyore* particularly irritating. What place did his skepticism leave for the victims? Millions of people were dying or suffering from hunger, an entire population was being deprived of its freedom, and his only concern was our credibility. We had risked our lives in fleeing. We had risked them in the camp. What more did we need to prove? The security agents never whispered a single word in our ears. When I had asked them for advice about how to conduct myself during the press conference, one of them suggested that I say whatever I feel—"only you may not want to tell them everything," he added, "or they might not believe you." We were anything but manipulated. The skepticism and insinuations of our interviewers left An-hyuk deeply shaken. He and a couple of the agents had tears in their eyes; this wasn't looking anything like a press conference rigged for propaganda purposes. Even some of the journalists were moved.

I decided to speak.

"If you don't want to believe us, go to the North! Do you think we risked our lives so we could come here and lie?"

A huge crowd was at the press conference. Never in my life had I spoken in front of so many people. Nonplussed by all the cameras and lights, I expressed only a fraction of what I wanted to. The next day, our story was in all the papers. The television and radio stations called us for interviews, and the Japanese and American press were interested. In time we got use to telling our story. Yet by repeating it so often, I occasionally felt I was trading my experience for a story that was no longer entirely my own.

스물둘

ADAPTING TO A
CAPITALIST WORLD

After our debriefing had wrapped up, we sat around waiting for someone to tell us what we should do next. Were we supposed to work? Could we go back to school? Boredom began setting in. The agents offered to rent us some videocassettes.

"Do you want action movies," they asked, "or erotic movies?"

"What are erotic movies?"

They explained that erotic movies were basically softcore porn, hardcore being illegal in South Korea. We opted for the erotic films—four in a row! One night seemed too short a time to make up for a lifetime of North Korean prudishness. We had entered a fairyland. We couldn't believe our eyes: What actors would play these roles? How could they get naked in front of the camera? We recalled the charges of debauchery we had heard leveled against the South. It was said, for example, that the Ehwa women's university was less a school for young women than for prostitutes, and that

225

these harlots actually slept—supreme act of debauchery—with American soldiers! In North Korea, it is unimaginable that a man should try to seduce a woman. Romantic adventures are unthinkable. And not only in the movies—in real life, too, the man is supposed to take the initiative in the most direct manner possible. Courtship is seen as a remnant of a bygone era, and love is never a real concern! Yet for all that, it is considered normal for a man to force a woman to give in to his advances.

We went out to the city, accompanied as before. South Korean authorities want to observe and keep track of renegades after they first arrive. They also want to protect them. The 1996 murder by Pyongyang agents of a high-ranking renegade with family connections to Kim Jong-il testified to the need for vigilance. Moreover, we needed their help. Finding our way through the megalopolis, dealing with public services, finding work: none of these is easy for people who have spent decades in the Hermit Kingdom, as North Korea is sometimes called.

After six months of continuous chaperoning, I was allowed to rent an apartment, and a local policeman was assigned to my case. When I needed to go out—to a press conference or an interview, to buy a refrigerator or to sign my lease—I called him and he accompanied me. After two years, I was allowed to live entirely on my own. The security agents' presence had been generally more helpful than burdensome. Despite the rage I often felt toward my guardian angel, I am indebted to him for the most fateful meeting of my life. He introduced me to a very rich businessman of Northern origin who had read my story in the papers and wanted to contribute 200,000 won ($200) a month toward my college tuition. He also bought me a computer and paid for programming lessons. More important, he taught me how to face hardships in my new world.

Then there was the Security Agency bureaucrat who first introduced me to the Protestant church that I still attend. Seoul's
Christian community offered me enormous material and emotional
support. Religion is very attractive to North Korean renegades. The
atmosphere of quasi-religious adoration in which we were raised in
North Korea only partially explains this phenomenon; more important, I believe, is the thirst for affection—for love, even—every
renegade feels. I don't know whether I am profoundly religious, but
I wanted to be baptized.

I was also lucky enough to receive support from a bank, which
gave me a scholarship for the duration of my studies. Add to that
the money I made from giving interviews and writing the occasional
article, and I had few material worries.

Since my integration into South Korean life ultimately would have
to take place through steady work, I joined Hanyang University. Its
founder, Kim Yon-jun, was a strong advocate for human rights in the
North. Many renegades had enrolled in his university, and I was
encouraged to do the same. I chose international business as my
major. All the students were much younger than I was, but they
accepted me as they might an older brother. They liked me a lot and
tried to help me however they could, especially with English, which
I spoke poorly. Despite our amicable relations, many things they did
put me off. They were always going out to cafés and restaurants, as
though getting a soda from the dispenser and lying on the grass
weren't good enough. They were throwing money out the window!
Life in the North had made me a bit of a Spartan. When students
sat down cross-legged in front of me and started smoking, I had a
hard time holding my tongue; you don't do that in front of someone
your senior. The North is hypertraditionalist. Friendships between
members of the opposite sex is not the norm. When a man speaks

to a woman his own age, he employs the familiar form of address, she the formal. Relations follow a strict hierarchy. Here, we were equal! Some of the female students were so self-confident, they hardly paid me any attention when I spoke to them.

I eventually got used to all this. I have fond memories of my days at the university, even though the leftist students often riled me. They always tried to make me see the shortfalls of the South Korean system of government. At least the North wasn't corrupted by a fierce, never-ending battle for profit! Though I lacked the theoretical arguments to counter their claims, I wasn't impressed. "Go to the North," I told my contradictors, "and you'll stop trying to excuse all Kim Il-sung's failures. Go find out for yourselves."

One day a discussion with a student member of Hanchongnyon, the university's leftist organization, grew rather heated. I was being bombarded with would-be intellectual arguments about class, domination, and imperialism, featuring references to people such as Pierre Bourdieu. Onlookers had surrounded us. Whose side were they on? Did they agree with my interlocutor when he said that I had a "subjectivist" point of view and that my personal experience was no basis for a global condemnation of North Korean politics? A couple of students later told me that the majority of spectators had been very touched by the story of my imprisonment and flight to China. I was glad to hear that: the original silence had been like a great invisible force. Leftist students would do well to consider the meaning of that silence.

My primary concern, though, had to do with my professional future. Despite the support of my fellow students, I struggled with English. From my end, I gave a lot of students financial help. Ironically, the North Korean renegade had become a well-off student, enjoying a free education, benefiting from handsome government subsidies, and earning fees from articles and speaking engagements. By contrast, many students from the South Korean provinces were surviving hand to mouth, living in tiny rented rooms, working—some as supermarket checkers, others as restaurant workers—and waiting for their parents to send them a little pocket money. I fed them and in several cases even paid their tuition. For me, it was a way of saying thank you.

With so much money on my hands, I slipped into an odd lifestyle in which I almost lost myself. Someone offered to rent me a new apartment in the upscale Changdam-dong neighborhood, a mixed office and live-in studio space, or *officitel*, as it's called in Seoul. I decided to take it. Here was an incredible universe in which money flowed like water. Out front one could see parked BMWs belonging to doctors, hostesses, movie stars. I didn't have a BMW, but I spent money with abandon, fascinated by the power it gave me, swooning in my success. I, a former prisoner, who had been reduced to killing rats for food and swallowing salamanders, was drinking with the people of this neighborhood and eating in their restaurants! I'd come a long way from being embarrassed by a young Chinese woman's invitation to dance. Now I was the one asking all the pretty girls to join me on the dance floor. At the same time, I was still a student. My night life and my studies were on a collision course. I came very close to being spoiled by all the money I received for opening my mouth! I no longer knew where I stood. I was uncomfortable with myself—and on certain early mornings, a little ashamed.

I made a clean break with that life. The desire to drown my sorrows didn't run as deep as other longings: to create stability in my life, to tell the world of the situation in North Korea, to help unfortunate refugees, and to find a wife to share the rest of my life. Yet here, too, a renegade encounters difficulties that never appear in government statistics and that no amount of money can solve. I recently fell in love with a girl from Seoul whom I would have been happy to marry, but in Korea, marriage isn't just a commitment between two individuals; it's the union of two families. Where was my family? Dead or infinitely removed. No family, no marriage. On top of that, how could her family not be suspicious of a North Korean? That my family and I paid handsomely for not assimilating into the North Korean regime mattered little. Familial prejudices are never easy to dismiss.

The citizens of South Korea should realize they have an important role to play in welcoming refugees. They aren't just people who have fled something; they are people who have a hard time adapting and a hard time forgetting what they have endured. I continue to have dreams in which I am running across the Yalu or in the mountains, North Korean security agents hot on my trail. They are about to catch me and I wake up covered in sweat. It is not enough for people to say they are for reunification. Their actions need to prove it. The rhetoric of reunification is one thing, people's attitudes toward North Korean renegades quite another. I don't question the South Korean population's desire for reunification, even though a large segment couldn't care less one way or another. What I do wish to denounce—based on my own experience—are the countless prejudices that are held against people from the North. Their poverty and economic inferiority are too often taken as a reflection of some natural inferiority. I myself have been the target of such misperceptions: whenever I dress elegantly, people look at me with suspicion. I'm not acting the way I'm expected to.

The same goes for work. Money is so important in South Korea, I always felt I would never be seen as equal unless I earned lots of money.

The South has a number of associations for North Korean renegades. One of them was founded by Ko Yong-hwan, a former North Korean diplomat stationed in Zaire. It seems to me that the group's main focus is helping wealthy renegades, who are already rather well adjusted. At the other end of the spectrum Hwang Jang-yop, the Worker's Party ideologue who fled North Korea in February 1997, created an association that tries to help all refugees while loudly proclaiming its hostility toward the Kim Il-sung dictatorship. Its sacred task—more important, according to its founder, than the battle against Japanese occupation—is to publicize the crimes committed in the North by Kim Jong-il. Hwang Jang-yop wants nothing less than to bring down the regime. This organization also raises money to help support and protect renegades wandering along the Chinese border.

Much remains to be done. Over the last ten years, the situation in North Korea has continued to deteriorate. Refugees now crossing into China over the Yalu, or farther east over the Tumen River, tell us terrible things about the conditions in North Korea. Eyewitness accounts gathered by Good Friends—a Buddhist-inspired association—are crushing. People have been reduced to eating grass and the bark of young pines and sycamores. Haggard children wander about with their skin often black and rotting from infection. As soon as the first cold spells hit, they die of typhoid fever or cholera. Families are being torn apart. Parents frequently abandon their youngest children in the hope that someone better off might find them and give them a home. People try to cross the border without means or protection. Whenever I hear these stories,

I think of all the advantages I had. Money allowed me to reach the border by train and to hire a guide.

Today, most refugees arrive at the riverbank exhausted by days and sometimes weeks of walking. The guards treat them harshly. No gifts? No pity! Myriad are the stories of vicious beatings and imprisonment in foul cells. Even if they manage to avoid the border guards, these unfortunates are not invited to dinner and karaoke after their crossing, as I was. The Chinese police often close their eyes to the illegal human traffic, but they also return a considerable number to North Korea. All along the border, Christian groups are doing incredible work to save the *kkot-jebi*—or wandering children—feeding and giving shelter to the neediest among them. These groups are also fighting against the trade in young North Korean women: 2,000 to 5,000 yuan is all a bride costs in this region of China.

I try to help newly arrived renegades integrate into their new universe. Sometimes I am solicited to give assistance to refugees hiding out in China. At the end of October 1999, a South Korean businessman who trades in China told me he passed my phone number along to two renegades who claimed to know me. A few days later, I got a telephone call from China. "Comrade Kang Chol-hwan," said the voice. That "comrade" (*dongmu*) was quite a throwback. There was a time when I heard and used that word constantly. The caller was the brother of a woman neighbor of ours at Yodok. I had met him once at his sister's. He began by giving me news of my sister, whom he last saw two years after my defection. "She had been interrogated, of course, and looked like she was very poor. The authorities seemed worried when they realized you were gone. They were afraid you would talk about the camp. During the morning lesson in our village your case was always being discussed. The party secretary told us that we all needed to be vigilant and make sure such incidents don't happen again, that we should feel responsible and speak out about any rumored plan of escape."

I also learned that several of my old friends, as well as a number of Party cadres involved in my case, had been sent to the camps. These included Yi Chang-ho, the local secretary, and Kim Jong-nam, the head of the Office for Public Security. Others, such as the director of security, the general secretary for administration, and the secretary of Party organization, were fired. I am sad I caused others to suffer. I am also sad that because of me, my sister lives under the shadow of constant threat. At the same time, I am proud that my escape filled the entire *gun* with a certain hope. As for the North Korean refugee who called me, it will be understood that the less detail I provide about his story, the better. For the sake of giving people a fuller picture of the difficulties renegades face, I will, however, mention that his Chinese runners threatened to turn him over to the police and sell off his young lady companion unless I sent him some money. Fortunately, the South Korean businessman who first put us in contact had a way of changing their minds. . . .

에필로그

EPILOGUE

Pursuing Aid for
North Korea

At present, I want to work on behalf of the unfortunate souls attempting to flee repression and famine. All of us, we and the government, must be more active. We are all brothers it seems, but our sisters are being bought and sold at the border. Are we to continue showing such restraint? The shortages in food, energy, and medicine are serious. According to anecdotal reports by journalists, there have been countless victims. Estimates are that famine will cause between 1 and 3 million deaths. No more accurate number is available, because no one has penetrated the North Korean bunker deeply enough to perform an adequate study. Anyone who has stood as I have beside a person slowly dying of hunger—who has seen this horror with his own eyes—will never linger to debate the pros and cons of food aid. The only real question is one of distribution. Who knows how much aid is siphoned off to buttress the army? One often hears such objections, even among people who want to see more food go to the North.

It's true that in North Korea the army comes first. But it is not a professional army cut off from the rest of the population. It is made up entirely of volunteers—legions upon legions of them. Frequently, the requests outnumber the openings. The backgrounds of the volunteers explains their enthusiasm. Many of them are the children of peasants, for whom the army is a first step to entering the Party. The poorest families enlist their children because they know they will get food and clothing there. The army also represents an opportunity to climb the social ladder: thirty percent of all veterans go on to enter the university.

Another argument against offering aid is that even when it's not diverted to the army, it allows the regime to save its foreign currency—which it should be spending on cereals—for weapons purchases and sumptuous feasts in honor of the country's leaders. Here is the dilemma one always faces when trying to help a population that has fallen victim to famine-causing political and economic systems: aiding the population also means maintaining the regime.

The question of aid, whether of food or anything else, is not primary; rather, priority should be given to receiving those who escape and according them protection under the law. More work also must be done to introduce the people of North Korea to the outside world, and the outside world to North Korea. International public opinion and world leaders should be pressed to become more conscious of the North Korean tragedy and to force Kim Jong-il to change his behavior or risk being condemned by an international court.

I did not join in the exaltation and enthusiasm shared by many South Koreans during the recent summit between North and South Korea. One has to be naive to believe that Kim Jong-il's smile and affability as a host signal any real change in a dictatorial regime without equal in the modern world—a place where the population has been kept in a constant state of terror for decades. If Kim Jong-il is smiling, it's because he is sure of his grip on power and plans to continue exercising it with the same contempt he has always had for the most basic of human rights.

Swimming against the tide of public opinion, I've attempted to explain—most notably in the July 2000 issue of the magazine *Chosun*—that Kim Jong-il's friendliness is calculated. His feigned desire for greater openness has the same end as his years of calculated reclusion: to deepen and expand his own mythification. I also explained that reunification with the North as it stands today is impossible. South Korea is a democratic country, a place where power lies with the people. In the North, people lead a pathetic existence given over entirely to the Party and Kim Jong-il, who confiscates power for his own ends. The only acceptable reunification is one that grants North Koreans the freedom to lead a life worthy of human beings. They are now dying of hunger without the right to utter a word of protest, crushed by a system that walks all over their fundamental human rights.

We are told that the answer to these little problems—the respect for human rights, the concentration camps, the kidnaping of South Korean and Japanese citizens—currently is not of primary concern. We are told that this debate would be better left for another day, that the North Koreans' lot should improve before we undertake reunification; but by then they'll all be dead!

Reunification is inevitable, but it can only take place once Pyongyang has stopped crucifying the population under its control. How can we stand by while troops of orphans cross the Yalu and Tumen rivers seeking refuge in China? How can we stand by while parents sell their daughters for something to eat? I don't want to see any more skeletal children with wide, frightened eyes. I don't want any more children sent to the camps and their mothers forced to divorce their fathers. I want their grandfathers to be around to tell them stories—and their giggles on the banks of the Daedong never to be interrupted by the arrival of bureaucrats from the Security Force.